Behind the Scenes
in **Versailles**

Pascal Bonafoux I Photography: Gilles Targat

CHÂTEAU DE VERSAILLES

chêne

Preface

A superficial visit of Versailles could reduce the palace into a prodigious series of rooms and halls, running from the chapel to the Queen's Staircase, the King's Apartment to the Hall of Mirrors, not forgetting the Queen's Apartment, upon which Marie-Antoinette had notably left her mark. However, the history of Versailles represents much more than that. It is a world apart. It is the palace that stretched, in an incredible span from the North wing to that of the South, some 680 metres. It is a royal residence that offers a masterly account of court life during the 17th and 18th Centuries. It is also where Louis-Philippe installed the great vestiges of France, as part of the museum of French history, within the palace built by Louis XIV. Versailles is also the gardens, making this an open-air palace, and the park, a descendant of the 'Grand Park' of the Ancien Régime. It is also the Trianons, and their particular gardens. It is the places of piety, with the palace chapel and those of the Trianon, as well as the places of pleasure, with the royal opera – thanks to Gabriel's genius – and that of the Small Trianon, conceived by Mique for she who would become known as 'The Austrian'.

Versailles is also, beyond the official representation, a knotted fabric of backstage scenes, a world of intimacy among kings and princes, and for those who served them, and surrounded them. This was common ground necessary for the functioning of a vast machine, that of Versailles, that provided the common living environment for several thousand people. Versailles is also the stage and backstage to so much major history; it was a military hospital for the Prussians who mounted a siege of Paris in 1870, it was the apotheosis of the German Empire in 1871, the site for the restoration of parliamentary life in France that had been interrupted by the defeat at Sedan and the strife of the Paris Commune, the home to treaties following the end of the First World War in 1918, and the stage to the Republic's pomp and ceremony for the world's great leaders under De Gaulle, Pompidou, Giscard d'Estaing and François Mitterrand. The wonderful book by Pascal Bonafoux explores with finesse just some of these scenes, behind the scene. It is an invitation to share a better understanding of this palace, which unites together both the glory of the century of Louis XIV and the constancy of French genius.

Thanks are given to the author, to whom I would like to signify my amicable admiration, and his publisher.

Jean-Jacques Aillagon
President of the museum and national domain of Versailles

Contents

Stage Right, the Gardens

Prologue

EVER SINCE AESCHYLUS AND SOPHOCLES, THE WORD 'PROLOGUE' — THAT PART OF A PLAY THAT PRECEDES THE ENTRANCE OF THE CHOIR — BELONGS TO THE LANGUAGE OF THEATRE. While it might at first appear out of place in the context of the palace of Versailles, it is in fact most appropriate. Because Versailles is a theatre where power, all its strength and its prestige are acted out on a stage. Just as King Louis XIV wished it, everywhere in Versailles is a theatrical scene; the gardens, the courtyards and every room in the palace.

FOR EVIDENCE of this, one needs only to read Scene Three of Molière's play *The Impromptu of Versailles*, the first presentation of which was held at Versailles, on October 14th, 1663, in front of Louis XIV. In his instructions to the actors, Molière says: "Note first of all that the scene is situated in the king's antechamber, for it is a place where, every day, rather agreeable things happen. It is easy to bring into it every person that one could want to..."* One after the other, all these people will be either in the choir or play such and such a part, but none will have the principle role. That is for the king. Louis XIV wanted Versailles to be a theatre and his intimate order to the dauphiness, just after her marriage, leaves no doubt about this. Referring to the thrice-weekly court receptions in the State Apartments, he told her: "Madam, I want there to be apartment [evenings] and that you dance there. We are not like ordinary people. We have a duty to give ourselves entirely to the public."*

TO THE PUBLIC... Everyone who enters the court at Versailles must become an actor there and Louis XIV is the first to know this. Primi Visconti, Count of Saint-Mayol, recounts: "Finding myself in his room with his courtesans, I noticed on several occasions that, if the door has by chance been opened, or if he leaves, he just as soon composes his attitude and adopts another facial expression, as if he should appear on a stage; in short, he knows how to be the king anywhere."* And he adds: "In public he says nothing and maintains his seriousness, because he has the gravity of a theatre king."* Marie-Antoinette's first lady-in-waiting, Madame Campan, testifies in a different manner how, under the reign of Louis XVI, Versailles had not ceased being a theatre. She was unhappy at the influence enjoyed by the abbot of Vermond, "that man who the unlucky star over Marie-Antoinette had reserved to lead her in her first steps upon the eminent and dangerous theatre that was the court of Versailles".*

Opposite page:
The crown above the Royal Gate in Versailles, re-built in 2007-2008 to the specifications of the original by Jules Hardouin-Mansart, which was destroyed in 1794.

THERE IS A SINGULAR paradox imposed upon Versailles; because all the places within the palace are scenes, each also has a role as the wings behind-the-scene... This means that the Hall of Mirrors is a theatre wing in the same manner as a hidden flight of stairs, just like that which is named 'the stairway of mistresses'... It also means that the Trianons, Grand and Petit, are scenes and wings, just like the Queen's hamlet, the Grand Stables and the vegetable garden.

CONCERNING THE REPERTOIRE, there is another singularity. Everything is brought together at Versailles, from comedy to tragedy, and even farce. And because within Versailles one must accept to become an actor, circumstances can lead the king himself to play a farcical role. For example, as when Louis XV secretly decides to go, incognito, to the Opera ball in Paris. He doesn't return to Versailles until six o'clock in the morning: "He had to pass by the apartments, which were locked and guarded. There was knocking at a door. The body guard demanded who was there, and was told: 'Open up, sentinel, it's the King.'— 'The King should be in bed at present, I won't open at all, and you won't pass through, whoever you are, unless there is light.' It was necessary to fetch light, after which the guard opened up and recognised the king. 'Sire,' exclaimed the sentinel, 'I ask your majesty to forgive me, but I am under orders to let no-one pass through here. Thus, please have the goodness to relieve me of my duty.' The King was most happy with the punctiliousness of his guard."

MADAME DE POMPADOUR never stopped having to learn roles. On Wednesday, December 11th, 1748, she sings the part of Herminie in Campra's opera *Tancrède*. The duke comments: "The most difficult parts are performed to perfection by Madame de Pompadour in such a manner that leaves nothing to be desired." Two days later, on Friday the 13th, acting in Philippe Quinault's play *La Mère coquette*, she "played the role of the lady-in-waiting, called Laurette." Needless to say, "the play was marvellously acted." On December 25th the duke records that, two days earlier, in a performance of *Baucis and Philemon*, it was the Viscount of Rohan who played Philemon and Madame de Pompadour who was Baucis... Finally, on January 15th, 1749, she played the part of the goddess of fruits Pomone in 'The Earth' scene of the opera-ballet *Les Éléments*.

HOW CAN ONE NOT BE AN ACTOR WITHIN THE COURT? Molière, in *The Impromptu of Versailles*, told the actor Brécourt: "you perform an honest courtier, like you have already done in *Critique of the School for Wives*, which means you must take on a calm demeanour, a natural tone of voice, and to gesticulate the least you can". But a few years later, he could have advised him, in 1688, to read *Les Caractères* by the French essayist Jean de La Bruyère. He would find the following: "A man who knows the [rules of] court is the master of his gestures, of his eyes, and of his face; he is profound and impenetrable; he conceals the bad offices, smiles at his enemies, restrains his moods, disguises his passions, denies his heart and speaks and acts against his true sentiments."* How can anyone achieve this without being an actor?

IN THE 18ᵀᴴ CENTURY, the Count of Tilly tells of having met at the court a grand lady capable of addressing a range of specific greetings "for women in waiting, one for women of quality, one for women of the court, one for titled women, one for women with a historic name; one for women born into a grand family but married to husbands below them, one for women who have exchanged through marriage their common names for a distinguished one, yet another for women who come from a good name of nobles of the gown, and finally another for those whose principal characteristic is to have a high-spending house which provides fine suppers."* She could have given precious advice to Mademoiselle Clairon – an actress with the Théâtre-Français, born in 1723, who was considered one of the greatest tragediennes of that century – for the writing of her *Memoirs* which included "Thoughts about dramatic art and theatrical declamation.".…

VERSAILLES, continued to be a theatre after October 6ᵗʰ, 1789, another singularity and that is not the least among them. That was the day when the people of Paris brought Louis XVI and his family to the capital after which no other monarch would again live in the palace. But that did not stop Versailles from remaining to be a theatre of power. It was in Versailles that Prussia's Wilhelm 1ˢᵗ became emperor of Germany. It was in Versailles that the presidents of the Third and Fourth Republics were elected. It is again at Versailles, ever since the beginning of the current Fifth Republic, that France's senators and parliamentary representatives continue to meet together to amend the constitution, at an event called the Congress.

IN THE 17ᵀᴴ CENTURY, La Bruyère wrote: "In 100 years the world will continue wholly as the same; it will be the same theatre and the same decorations, but there will not be the same actors."* More than two centuries later, the theatre that is Versailles remains unchanged…although the "decorations" are no longer the same. The Revolution has cast aside a symbol of absolute monarchy, Napoleon modified the Grand Trianon, and king Louis-Philippe 1ˢᵗ dedicated the palace "to all the glories of France." The Third Republic installed parliament there, and under the Fourth and Fifth Republics there has been constant restoration work upon both the palace building and its gardens. For if Versailles has never ceased being a theatre, it has also always been a building site. An example: in 1752, the Ambassadors Stairway was destroyed. Work on its replacement, designed by architect Ange-Jacques Gabriel, began in 1772 but was not finished until…1985.

BECAUSE VERSAILLES contains such a rich history of so many different periods and epochs, behind the scenes are more theatres, those of shadows, where Molière while in rehearsals appears to be conversing with Georges Clemenceau as he signs the 1919 World War I peace treaty; where Casanova, who had come to propose to the king the idea of creating a lottery, meets the sculptor Pierre Puget, whose masterpiece the *Milo of Croton* was erected in the park; where king Louis-Philippe 1ˢᵗ, as he checks upon progress with the work on the Hall of Crusades, takes pity on a young Englishman who arrived at the palace in 1749 and who, the Duke of Luynes records, "has not a disagreeable face" and about whom "it is said that he had a great passion of the heart and that he came here to heal himself of an illness that the English call spleen"*; where Pope Pius VII, forced by Napoleon to travel to France to crown him as emperor, appears to bless the Count of Chalmazel. The latter has just met, in the staircase, "some people he knows and who ask him where he is going: – 'to the Bull's-Eye' he replies. – 'There's no-one and we can assure you that's the case, because we've just left there.' – 'I don't care. I will always hear what's said in there."

IT IS THESE 'ANACHRONISTIC' VOICES "anachroniques" that hover to one's ears in the wings of Versailles.

ENTER. •

Opposite page:
A series of doors in the Private Apartments.

All quotes marked with an asterisk are modern translations by the publisher.*

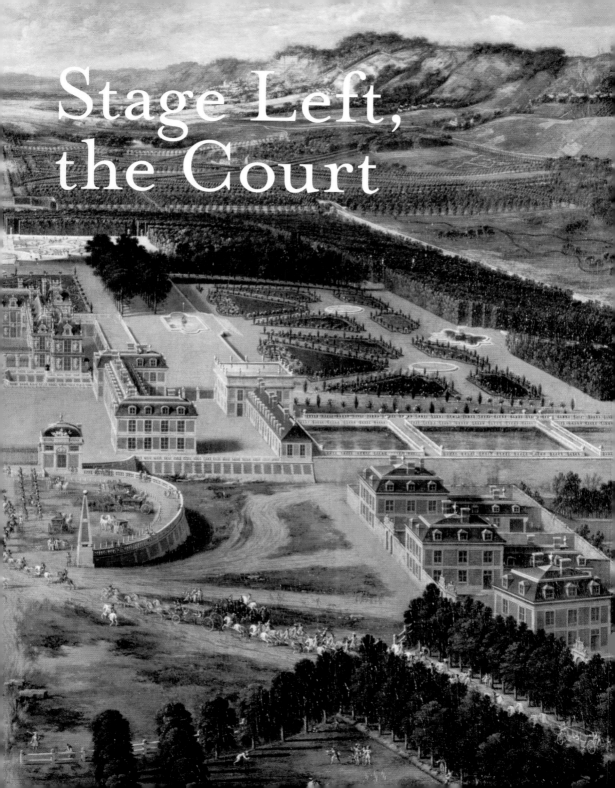

Stage Left,
the Court

Act One,
The Bourbons

IF VERSAILLES IS A THEATRE, THEN 'THE BOURBONS' IS THE TITLE OF THE FIRST ACT OF THE PERFORMANCE. THE STAGE CURTAIN ROSE ON MAY 7ᵀᴴ, **1664** AND FELL FINALLY ON OCTOBER 6ᵀᴴ, **1789**.

LOUIS XIV, was 25 years-old when he brought all of his court together at Versailles for the first time. He was host to some 600 people and the entertainment provided, like all other services offered to the guests, had to be faultless. Thus "from Paris came an endless number of people needed for the dancing and the acting, together with craftsmen of all sorts, so many in fact that they resembled a small army,"* recorded a 1682 booklet describing the event, published by Robert Ballard, 'the only printer for music'. It was, of course, most certainly not down to luck that it never rained during the partying, which went on until May 14ᵗʰ. "The sky itself appeared to favour the plans of his majesty (...) in order to show that the planning and power of the king were able to resist the greatest of inconveniences."*

MONSIEUR DE VIGARINI and the Duke of Saint-Aignan chose, with the king's agreement, the palace of Alcides as depicted by the Italian poet Ludovico Ariosto to be the theme of the festivities, which were entitled '*The Pleasures of the Enchanted Isle*'. According to the story, Angelica's ring has the power to ward off the enchantments which keep the knight Rogero and his companions in the palace of the magician, which Melissa finally slips onto Rogero's finger. It is the king himself who plays Rogero. He appears on May 7ᵗʰ "mounted on one of the most beautiful horses in the world, the flame-coloured saddlery of which sparkled with gold, silver and fine stones; His Majesty was armed in the Greek manner (...)and wore body armour of silver blades, covered in a rich embroidery of gold and diamonds." The appearance of the king is so remarkable that "he eclipses the brilliance of ancient heroes." It is Molière who plays the court jester to the Princess of Elis. On Sunday, May 11ᵗʰ, his comedy *The Impertinents*, with opening and ballet, is played out in the hall of the palace. The next day he presents the

Rupture du Palais et des enchantemens de l'Isle   Troisiesme Journée   d'Alcine representeé par un feü d'Artifice

Preceding double page:
Château de Versailles, by Pierre Patel, 1668.
Above:
The Pleasures of the Enchanted Isle,
by Israël Silvestre, 1664.

Right:
*Greeting the Ladies,
C17th engraving.*

first three acts of his unfinished play *Tartuffe*, and on May 13th he mounts a performance of *The Forced Marriage*. On May 14th, with no further resources for entertaining the courtesans and because Versailles had already then begun to be the most interminable building site of his reign, the king left for Fontainebleau. As a souvenir for posterity, a book was commissioned to record all the magnificent events, from the cavalry parades to the fireworks, from the ballets to the comedies. This 91-page folio edition included nine engravings by Israël Silvestre.

On October 5th 1789, as night fell, a large and angry crowd gathered below the windows of the bedroom of King Louis XVI. Those who had begun assembling at around four o'clock in the afternoon had forced the two main gates. Beyond the Marble Courtyard, a crowd formed on the place d'Armes, in front of the Grand and Small Stables, before a rainstorm began dispersing some of them. During the evening, the Marquis de La Fayette arrived, greeted by a courtesan who exclaimed "Oh, here comes Cromwell!" to which La Fayette answered: "Cromwell would not have entered alone."

He insisted he could maintain order, and at two o'clock in the morning, the king and queen retired to their apartments. When dawn came, the shout of a guard ripped through the silence: "Save the queen!" A crowd had invaded the palace, entering by the Courtyard of Princes, and murdered several guards before the queen manages to flee through a hidden door. Several hours then passed before a delegation of representatives of the national assembly, including its president Jean-Joseph Mounier, arrive at the court accompanied by several women. More hours pass.

LA FAYETTE convinced the queen to present herself with him on the balcony, from where he succeeded in silencing the crowd below. "The queen is angry to see what she sees in front of her eyes," he told them. "She was misled. She promises that will not happen again. She promises to

Below:
The French Revolution: the vanguard of women on their way to Versailles on October 5th, 1789 (second day of the Sans-culottes) 1789.

La Journée memorable de Versailles le lundi 5 Octobre 1789.

Dans cette émeute generale plusieurs Gardes du Corps ont été Massacrés deux
dentre eux furent Decolés et leurs tetes portées en Triomphe par ce meme peuple
ami de la liberté Nationale.

love her people, to be bound to them in the same way as Jesus Christ is to his church!"* The crowd began cheering loudly, just as strongly as, afew moments earlier, they had been shouting their hate. The queen, in tears, retired. The crowd remained in position before Monsieur de Guiche appeared and announced that the king was ready to meet with some of the women among them who had entered the palace. Those closest to the door are summoned, among them Louison Chabry, a young woman in her twenties. Brought before the king, she stammered and mumbled as he questioned her, and answered 'no' when he asks if she had wanted to harm the queen, before fainting. As she came around, she was comforted and escorted away. Outside, she recounted the kindly words of the king to the crowd, which become furious with her, accusing her of being bought, and threatening to hang her. A group of soldiers bring her to safety and lead her back before the king. He agreed to return to the balcony to convince the crowd that she did not receive a single coin. Once back inside, the king orders a court carriage to accompany Louison Chabry home to Paris.

At the end of the morning, it was clear that the royal family would not accede to the crowd's demand that they never return to Paris. The orders are given; "You will remain the master here," Louis xvi tells his Minister of War, the Marquis de La Tour du Pin, "Make sure you preserve my poor Versailles."* A few moments later, on that October 6th 1789, the convoy, carrying Louis xvi, left Versailles. Perhaps, as he rode towards Paris in the carriage, surrounded by rioters bearing poles adorned with the hacked-off heads of royal guardsmen, he thought back to May 10th 1774. Then, just a few hours before the death of Louis xv, before the cry went up "the king is dead, long live the king!", he murmured: "It seems to me that the universe will fall upon me."

Opposite page:
*The memorable day
of Versailles, Monday
October 5th, 1789:
the people carry the
heads of the massacred
Guardsmen, 1789.*

Left:
The Marble Courtyard.

The Œil-de-Bœuf

In 1701, it was in the line of the castle, within the main building built by his father Louis XIII, that the king gave orders for his room to be re-built. No-one could any longer doubt the symbol that the whole palace had become: it was clear that everything converged towards the king. This new disposition involved the destruction of the wall that separated the bedchamber he had occupied since 1684 from the room called the 'salon des Bassans' (so-named because it contained the paintings of Italian painter Jacopo da Ponte, known as Jacopo Bassano the Elder, and others by his four sons). Because the ceilings of the two rooms were not of the same height, the roofing was raised. A bull's-eye (œil -de-bœuf) window was installed, looking out onto the Queen's court-yard, to allow light into the antechamber where numerous courtesans

Opposite page:
A detail of the decorations of the Œil-de-Bœuf Salon.
Below:
View of the Queen's Courtyard from the Œil-de-Bœuf Salon.

would gather to await the Grand Lever du Roi (the king's formal awakening). This very particular addition immediately lent its name to the room. During the last 14 years of the reign of Louis XIV, the Œil-de-Bœuf thus became the place where one would prepare to meet the sovereign, he who the son of English king James II described as "born with an air of majesty so imposing to everyone that one could not approach him without being gripped by fear and respect."*

No-doubt the only one to be indifferent to such intimidation were the gilded sculptures of children who, the king had insisted, should be the subject of the decorations of the frieze surrounding the attic. Several sculptors – Poirier, Hardy, Flamen, Hurtrelle, Van Clève – were commissioned to model child subjects in the Orangery that was emptied, during the summer, of its trees. The sculptures variously depicted the children in front of a trellis, playing with garlands, with dogs and with musical instruments. It is within this room that the courtesans prepared themselves for the only exercise that was suited to the court of Louis the Great. The Duke of Saint-Simon cuttingly described it thus: "Suppleness, lowness, an admiring manner, dependent, grovelling more than anything, giving the impression of being nothing without him, were the only ways of pleasing him."*

The habits of the place never changed; the Count d'Hézecques, who was a court page during the last three years of the reign at Versailles of Louis XVI, from 1786 to 1789, described the Œil-de-Bœuf Salon as follows: "It was a temple of ambition, of intrigue and falseness."*

Opposite page:
View of the Œil-de-
Bœuf from the Queen's
Courtyard.

Theatre within theatre...

VERSAILLES MUST BE APPROACHED WITH CAUTION...

THAT WAS A WELL KNOWN fact in the 17ᵗʰ Century, when the essayist La Bruyère wrote: "The province is the place where the court, as from its own point of view, appears as something admirable; if one gets close to it, the attractiveness diminishes, like things of a perspective that one looks at too closely."* To have come to Versailles, to have seen the court at close hand, changes nothing. The dramatist and writer Louis Sébastien Mercier, who in 1781 published the first volumes of his *Tableau de Paris* (Portrait of Paris), warned that anyone "who returned to his provincial home place relayed an insolent and ridiculous story on the sovereign's stay. He has seen the king, the princesses, the grand suppers, nothing less true. But he adds untruthful circumstances, which are received with ignorant admiration and credulity. There is licence for exaggeration and the most bizarre of tales is heard out. The storyteller can persuade the other of anything he wants."*

OTHERS WHO RECOUNT Versailles, from the Duke of Saint-Simon to Madame Campan, – Marie-Antoinette's first lady-in-waiting – and including the Duke of Luynes, who wrote his *Memoirs* about the reign of Louis xv, the Count of Ségur and the Abbot of Choisy, do indeed tell their own 'most bizarre of tales', despite their scruples. But how could they not recount what they saw, heard and said? Their accounts, it should be remembered, are of what was in effect a show, a performance. At Versailles, one must recognise the skills of the stagehands and beware of that *deus ex machina* who never, ever shies from intervening...

ANOTHER REASON RAISON for being cautious is detailed, once again, in the *Tableau de Paris* by Louis Sébastien Mercier: "There is nothing that disgusts so much in art as that which is revealed in the wings; imagination is disenchanted (...) How dramatic art is wonderful when one is seated in the stalls! How hideous it is when one appraises it from the wings among

Above:
The stage and the wings
of the Queen's Theatre in the Petit Trianon.

the accessories that make it work! (...) One must lose the wings from one's sight; one must even forget them in order to begin a new work. That he who adores art and who doesn't want to lose the exquisite sentiment it provides, abstains from watching the anatomic game of our performances; there is matter there to heal the ardour of the most intrepid enthusiasts of Melpomene and Thalia."*

WE MAY BE more concerned in this text by Clio, the Greek muse of history, but nevertheless the above-mentioned muses are relevant because Versailles – the court of Versailles – is a theatre. It is so by the very will of the king. In his memoirs written for the dauphin, Louis XIV describes the court he wanted: "This society of pleasures, which gives to the people of the court an honest familiarity with us, which touches them and charms them more than we can say. The people, on the other hand, are pleased by the spectacle, where at heart we always have the aim of pleasing them; and all our subjects, in general, are delighted that we enjoy what they enjoy, or at what they succeed in doing best. By that we have hold of their spirit and their heart, sometimes perhaps more than by compensations and well-doings"*

THE SAME APPLIES to foreigners. The king adds: "(...) in a State that they see as flourishing and well-ordered, what is consumed in this spending which could appear superfluous has for effect upon them a very advantageous impression of magnificence, of power, of richness and grandeur; this without counting also that by partaking in all the corporal exercises that can only be enjoyed and maintained by all this, always places the prince in good favour and makes for advantageous judgement of what one doesn't see, by what one does see."* The king's last words here are key. Because the notion of 'advantageous judgement of what one doesn't see, by what one does see' raises the suspicion that what is not seen may not be to the advantage of what one is given to see. If for nothing else than because the principal reason for being at the court styled by Louis XIV is to have hold of spirits and hearts. Within the theatre of Versailles, upon the stage as in the wings, perhaps there is little other than politics that matter.

WHICH IS PERHAPS what is illustrated in the plays that were performed there. On September 17ᵗʰ, 1672, Molière staged at Versailles a production of *The Learned Women*. When, in Act Five, the audience hears the phrase "I said it, I want it; don't answer me back"* each of them could imagine it was the king speaking. That this alexandrine is spoken by Philamente, wife of Chrysale, described as a fine bourgeois, is of little importance. It was a different story when Brutus was staged there one day in 1730. The Count of Ségur was unable to forget the moment: "(...) I always remember the astonishment with which I heard, in the performance hall of the palace of Versailles, all the court enthusiastically applauding Voltaire's tragedy Brutus, and in particular these two lines: "I am the son of Brutus, and upon my heart / is engraved liberty and the horror of kings."

WHAT A SINGULAR PLACE Versailles was. One where, theatre within theatre, the comedies and tragedies performed there provide — or steal — the lines of history.

"The room of Madam the Dauphiness and that also of the Queen are alternately public and private, because at lunch everyone enters and in the evening there are only invitations."* Duke of Luynes

Molière, Racine and Mozart

MOLIÈRE WAS AMONG THOSE WHO, WITH THE PERORMANCE OF '*THE PRINCESS OF ELIS* ON MAY 8TH **1664** AND THAT OF '*TARTUFFE*', FOUR DAYS LATER ON THE **12**TH , TOOK PART IN THE *PLEASURES OF THE ENCHANTED ISLE*, THE EVENT WHICH MARKED THE BEGINNING OF THE HISTORY OF VERSAILLES. When he was presented before the king by the Duke of Créqui on February 28th, 1664, the sovereign accepted to be godfather to the playwright's first son. The king provided Molière's theatre company with a grant of 7,000 livres and decreed that the players should become the king's troupe. Did Louis XIV, in thanks for providing the king with laughter, ever invite Molière to his dinner table? Moreover, did he invite him to read there the sonnet about the conquest of the Franche-Comté in February, 1688, that the playwright dedicated to the king? The sovereign would not

Below:
Molière at the table of Louis XIV, Jean-Auguste-Dominique Ingres, 1857.

have been indifferent to the smiling tercets: "Do not wait, upon returning from such a wonderful enterprise / The attentions of our muse with a brilliant homage / This exploit demands one, it must be said / But our songs, Great King, are not ready soon enough / And you take less time to carry out your conquests / Than is needed to properly praise them."* But, for the painter Jean-Auguste-Dominique Ingres it was of little importance whether or not Louis XIV did actually invite Molière to his table in a room which far from resembled that depicted in his painting of 1857.

Below:
Racine reading from Athalie before Louis XIV and Madame de Maintenon, Julie Philipaut, 1819.

THE SON of the 17ᵗʰ Century dramatist Jean Racine records a number of interesting details about the life and works of his father in his *Memoirs*,

Above:

Mozart received by Madame de Pompadour, 1763, coloured wood engraving circa 1890, after the painting by Vincente Paredes.

published in 1747. In the work, Louis Racine quotes from *The Memoirs of the Countess of Caylus*, who tells of how Madame de Maintenon brought from Saint-Cyr to Versailles "once or twice, actresses to play in her room before the King, in their ordinary clothes" a performance of the second sacred tragedy *Athalie*, which she had commissioned from Racine. No doubt, she would have remembered if it had it been the author himself who read his work before the king. To which lines is she drawing the attention of Louis XIV? Perhaps those of Scene II, Act I, which appear to describe her situation: "In this place he allows me to be sovereign mistress."* Or, maybe, upon those words pronounced by Salomith in Scene VIII, Act III, which ring out like a condemnation: "Alas! In a court where there are no other laws / Except those of force and violence / Where the honours and employments / Are the price of a blind and lowly obedience."* Or perhaps the following two verses from Scene III, Act IV: "Of absolute power you ignore its intoxication / And of cowardly flatterers, the voice of enchantment."* This was no doubt the least of questions asked by Julie Philipaut, who painted this canvas in 1819.

ON FEBRUARY 12ᵀᴴ, 1764, Denis Pierre Jean Papillon de La Ferté, who by then had for seven years occupied the post of Commissioner for Entertainment and Ceremonies (it was his role to manage official ceremonies, festivities, balls, performances and even funerals), brought a young boy to the ladies' apartments. The child, born on January 27ᵗʰ, 1756, was just eight years-old, and was lodged, during his visit to Versailles with his father Leopold, at the Auberge du Cormier on the rue des Bons-Enfants. His name was Wolfgang Amadeus Mozart. Ever since Baron von Grimm arrived in Paris on November 18ᵗʰ, 1763, the German writer had constantly tried to present the young prodigy to high circles. He was indeed so successful in his enterprise that the infant composer – who had dedicated his first sonatas to Madame Victoire, daughter of Louis xv (and which were immediately published by Leopold) – was invited to join the king at a Grand Couvert (the large dinner service). During the dinner, Mozart conversed with the king in German. Why, indeed, would Madame de Pompadour not have wished to meet this child before whom all at the court were held in wonder? Leopold Mozart noted that "in a very haughty manner (...) she rules over everything, and still now."* A short while after this encounter, on May 15ᵗʰ, Madame de Pompadour was struck down by a congestion of the lungs. Of course, Vicente Garcia de Parades, who at the end of the 19ᵗʰ Century painted the Mozart we see here – bending to kiss Madame Pompadour's hand – was not a witness to the event. It is a piece of fiction, just as are, also, these following lines, placed in Mozart's mouth by French playwright Alexandre Picot, again at the end of the 19ᵗʰ Century in his play in one act and verse, *Mozart in Paris*: The audience was delirious / And what happened I cannot say / Presents and kisses fell upon me / When the king was called to embrace me / Princesses also hugged me / And I heard voices, soft and enchanting / Which hailed with passion my burgeoning merits / And I breathed in the heady incense of all this praise.

THE POWER OF VERSAILLES is such that everything there can become a theatre of memories...transformed into dreams and falsehoods.

Left:
Versailles,
F. Prudhomme, 1920, ,
after an original by
P.D. Martin, 1722.

Bourbon,
a name of power(s)

ONLY THREE BOURBONS RESIDED WITH THEIR COURTS AT VERSAILLES; LOUIS XIV, LOUIS XV AND LOUIS XVI.

LOUIS XIV (1638-1715) is the first among them. Son of Louis XIII (1601-1643), who built the first palace at Versailles, and of Anne of Austria, he was the third Bourbon to sit on the French throne. His grandfather, Henry III, King of Navarre, was King of France under the title Henry IV (1553-1610) after he succeeded Henry III of France, who designated him as the future king on his deathbed. But he only, at last, became monarch after he was made to abjure Protestantism in the basilica of Saint-Denis on July 25th, 1593. It was thus the grandfather of Louis XIV who founded the Bourbon dynasty, taking over from that of the Valois which had reigned over France, from Philip VI to Henry II, between 1328 to 1589.

LOUIS XV (1710-1774) would never have taken the throne but for a number of 'ifs': if the great dauphin, Louis (Monseigneur) of France, born in 1661 and eldest son of Louis XIV and Maria Theresa of Austria, had not died in 1711. Nor if Louis of France, Duke of Brittany, born in 1682 and second son of the Duke of Burgundy and Maria Anna Christina of Bavaria, and who became the dauphin in 1711, had not died in 1712. Nor, yet again, if there had not been the death a few months afterwards of Louis of France, Duke of Brittany, the second son of the Duke of Burgundy and Marie-Adélaïde of Savoy, born in 1707 and who had become the dauphin on the death of his father in 1712. Thus it was that the deaths of the son, grandson, the first and the second great-grandsons of Louis XIV made the Duke of Anjou, born in 1710, a dauphin in 1712 — and finally, following the death of Louis XV in 1715, a king.

LOUIS XVI (1754-1793) also would never have reigned if...the dauphin Louis of France, the first son of Louis XV, born in 1729 after his mother Maria Leszczynska had brought into the world Elisabeth, Henriette and Marie-Louise, had not died in 1765. Nor if the latter's first son, Louis Joseph Xavier, Duke of Burgundy, born in 1751, had not died in 1761, (before his

Opposite page:
Louis XIV, King of France,
Hyacinthe Rigaud, 1701.

10th birthday). Neither would he have taken the throne without the death in infancy in 1754 of Xavier Marie Joseph, Duke of Aquitaine, who was born in 1753. Thus the deaths of his elder brothers in 1754 and 1761, followed by that of his father in 1765, made the Duke of Berry the dauphin. He became king upon the death of his grandfather Louis XV in 1774, four years after he had married Marie-Antoinette, Archduchess of Austria.

THERE IS NO DOUBT, that Versailles is a symbol of the power of the Bourbons. Louis V Joseph de Bourbon-Condé, the eighth Prince of Condé, a prince by blood and born in Paris in 1736 and who died in 1818, is also a Bourbon. It is at Versailles that he married, on May 3rd, 1753, Charlotte de Rohan-Soubise. After the storming of the Bastille prison fortress in Paris, on July 14th, 1789, he was one of the first to flee in exile. His post as Grand Master of the House of the King had become a danger. The last thought on his mind was the fate of his childhood friend the Marquis de Sade, child of a lady-in-waiting to his mother and for whose son he was godfather. The marquis had been transferred from the Bastille towards another prison just days before July 14th. The Prince of Condé did not return to France until the Restoration, in 1814. That was when he took up his old quarters at the Bourbon Palace, situated on the Paris left bank and now home to the French parliament, upon which he had begun extension work in 1764. The architects Jacques-Pierre Gisors and Emmanuel-Chérubin Leconte had modified the building, nationalised in 1791, for sittings of the Council of Five Hundred between 1795 and 1799, a lower house legislative assembly set up after the Revolution. The authorities under the Restoration allowed him to return there, on condition that he rent it to the National Assembly (parliament).

Opposite page:
*Louis XV King of France
and Navarre, in
his great royal cloak
in 1760,* Jean Martial
Fredou after an original
by Louis-Michel Van Loo,
1763.

THAT IS HOW it was that the representatives of parliament under the Third Republic (1870 – 1940), after having sat at the palace of the Bourbons that was Versailles, returned to Paris, in 1879, to sit at...the Bourbon Palace. And it is thus that, during the Congress meetings, along with the senators of France, the same parliamentary representatives travelled from the

Palais-Bourbon, seat of legislative power, to elect the presidents of France's Third and Fourth Republics at Versailles. Since the beginning of the current Fifth Republic, it is also at Versailles, once the seat of absolute power, where the representatives meet to agree upon amendments to the constitution. In France, to this day, the name Bourbon remains associated with power.

Below:
Louis-Joseph de Bourbon, 8th Prince of Condé (1736-1818), Louis-Pierre Deseine, 1817.
Opposite page:
Louis XVI wearing the royal cloak and the order of the Saint-Esprit, Antoine-François Callet, 1779.

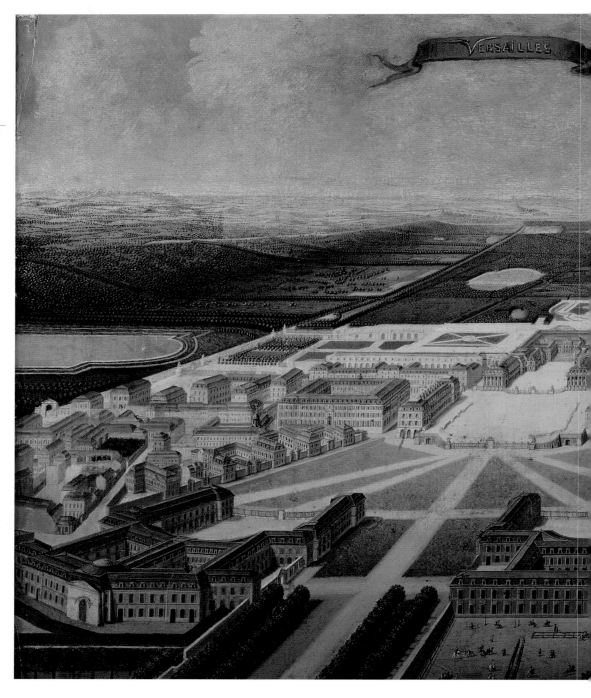

Left:
*Panoramic view
of Versailles,*
circa 1710-1715.

The letters of Versailles

AT THE EXTERIOR OF THE SAINT-LOUIS CHAPEL, SITTING UNDER, AND PERPENDICULAR TO, THE CANOPY, ARE A SERIES OF CROWNED 'L'S BACKED BY CROSSED PALM LEAVES. They stand for Louis xiv, just like the others 'L's that adorn the grills surrounding the choir area within the chapel. The chapel was the fifth and the last of those built for the palace since 1672. For the Duke of Saint-Simon, it "has about it everywhere the sad representation of a gigantic catafalque." The architect Jules Hardouin-Mansart began work on the building, the last of all the constructions under Louis xiv, in 1689. The project was interrupted by wars and was only finished on June 5th, 1710, after Robert de Cotte took charge following Hardouin-Mansart's death in 1708. Saint-Simon provides another acerbic observation: "The workmanship is exquisite in every detail, but the plan is worth nothing. Everything was centred on the gallery, because the king was never below."* Louis xiv died in 1715, but the 'L's continued to honour the kings Louis xv and xvi – who themselves had occasion to visit "below".

ANOTHER MONOGRAM appeared at Versailles not long after August 15th, 1774. That was the day when Louis xvi gave to Marie-Antoinette the key to the Small Trianon, upon which was encrusted 531 diamonds. For the first time in centuries, a French queen had become the owner of her palace. She hurried to place her own initials on the building – the work of Jacques Ange Gabriel for Louis xv (and also for Madame de Pompadour, who would never see it finished) – and on the staircase, where the crossed letters of 'M' and 'A' can be seen. Neither Pauline Borghèse, sister of Emperor Napoleon 1st, nor the latter's wife Marie-Louise, and neither Emperess Eugénie, who all had lived there, ever had them removed.

THUS IT WAS an 'L' which opened the history of the monarchy at Versailles, while the curtain went down on an 'M' and an 'A'.

Opposite page, clockwise from top: The frieze of the Saint-Louis Chapel, a detail from the choir gate of the Saint-Louis Chapel and *Portrait of the architect Jules Hardouin-Mansart,* Joseph Vivien, 1695.

Above:
Le monogram
of Marie-Antoinette, as
featured on decorations
of the Theatre of the
Queen in the Small
Trianon.

IT WAS THE REPUBLIC E that marked Versailles with yet another monogram. On September 4ᵗʰ, 1870, the Legislative Assembly proclaimed the end of the Empire, and the beginning of the Third Republic. But elections held in January 1871 returned a monarchist majority. As advancing Prussian troops threatened Paris, the members of parliament, returning from their exile in Bordeaux, met together in the royal Opera, built on May 16ᵗʰ, 1770 for the marriage between the dauphin and Marie-Antoinette. It was on May 26ᵗʰ, 1871, following a constitutional law passed on February 25ᵗʰ that established the two legislative chambers, that the members of parliament were attributed the aile du midi (south-facing wing) of the palace. The architect Edmond de Joly succeeded in building the new chamber within eight months. It was there, in the lunettes that surrounded the hall, above the cornice, he had inscribed two letters, both 'F's; they designated 'France', and were set back-to-back. For 'Republic', things would have to wait. These were uncertain times, when the Count of Chambord or Philip of Orleans could have taken the throne, or the imperial prince win the day. And the doubts persisted despite the election as president, on May 24th, 1873, of Patrice de Mac Mahon, who succeeded Adolphe Thiers (who had held the post since August 31st, 1871). It was thus that a simple 'F' would, for now, find agreement with everyone.

WHEN THE THIRD REPUBLIC EVENTUALLY found its feet, a painting was hung above the assembly president's seat depicting the opening session of the Estates-General of 1789, in the hall of Menus Plaisirs (the hall of general entertainment and ceremony). Jacques Necker, finance minister under Louis XVI, stands before the Third Estate to deliver his speech. Behind him, sitting on a throne, sits the king, wearing a hat bordered with white feathers. How paradoxical it is that it was therefore in front of the figure Louis XVI that the Third and Fourth Republics elected their presidents, while sitting at Congress; just as the Fifth Republic, following the introduction of presidential elections by universal suffrage, continues

Below:
The lunettes in the cornice of the hall of Parliament.

to meet before him at Congress sessions to modify the constitution. Further still, the 'R' remains missing from the lunettes. A cartoon in the former daily newspaper *Petit Journal*, dated January 12th, 1913, appears to refer to this. The scene is the meeting of the Congress at Versailles to elect a president to succeed Armand Fallières (and which finally elected, on January 17th, Raymond Poincaré), and introduces a female character representing the Republic itself, who forces open the doors to the hall. She carries a red, white and blue shield upon which are stamped the letters 'R' (for 'République') and 'F' (for 'Française'). She shouts out to the members of Congress: "Think of me first!"

Opposite:
"Think of me first!" cries France to the Congress meeting in Versailles, cartoon from the Petit Journal, 1913.
Below:
The floor of Congress.

Gentlemen, the King!

IT WAS AFTER THE DEATH OF CARDINAL DE MAZARIN THAT LOUIS XIV TOOK POWER, AGED 22. In his memoirs, the Duke of Choisy writes that "his spirit, hidden until then behind an outward appearance of naive kindness, was entirely revealed; he changed the order in his affairs."* In *Records of the Council*, the Count of Brienne notes for March 11, 1661: "The King had, the day before, brought together, in the room of the queen mother, before whom the councils were held [...] princes, dukes and ministers of State [...] to hear from his own mouth that he had taken the decision to command his State himself, without calling on any other help (those were his own terms) and in a very honest manner dispersed them, while telling them that, when he needed their good advice, he would call for them."*

MANY YEARS LATER, in his *Memoirs for the Instruction of the Dauphin*, the king confirmed what had been his resolution: "As for people who should have assisted my tasks, I decided that, for all things, I would not take a prime minister. And if you believe me, my son, as all of your successors after you, the name will be forever abolished in France, there being nothing more undignified than having, on one side, all the functions while, on the other side, is the king only in title."* This will of the king is the founding reason for creating Versailles. The palace and its dependencies must be the theatre where everyone is made fully aware that there is not, and there can never be, any other power than that of the king; the architecture and the festivities, the governance of the town and the protocol of the palace, the splendour of the decorations in the apartments and the masterly display of the fountains in the gardens. Everything contributes to the message. In *The Age of Louis XIV*, Voltaire wrote: "All that these things gave to the court of Louis XIV an air of grandeur that eclipsed all the other Courts of Europe. He was desirous that this lustre annexed to his person, should be reflected on all around him; that all the great should be honoured, but none of them powerful, beginning with his brother, and Monsieur le Prince."

Opposite page:
*Full portrait of
Louis XIV, King of France
and Navarre,* after
Claude Lefebvre, 1670.

THIS ABSOLUTE POWER of the king imposed that he should be informed of everything, and see everything. He missed no detail in Versailles, as Saint-Simon observed: "His eyes cast left and right at his wakening, his retiring, his meals, while passing through his apartments, in the gardens of Versailles where only the courtiers were allowed to follow him. He saw, and remarked upon, everyone. No-one escaped him, including those who hoped not to be seen [...] Louis XIV took great trouble to be well informed of all that was happening everywhere, in public places, in private homes, in international trade, within the secrets of families and those of relationships. The spies and reporters were infinite."* These last-mentioned are everywhere behind the scenes at Versailles. The reign of Louis XIV is also marked by suspicion. No allegory about mistrust is represented at Versailles, but the subject is well-understood by all. The king's sister-in-law, in 1706, wrote: "Among all the courts one is suspicious and letters are read, unless they are delivered to you by hand."

IF THE THEOLOGIAN, poet and writer François Fénelon demanded that the king know everything about his kingdom, that he knew the number of his subjects, labourers, craftsmen, etc., it was, he said, because: "A king who ignores all these things is only a half-king. His ignorance makes him incapable of putting right what has gone wrong. His ignorance is more harmful than the corruption among those men who govern below him."* But if Louis XIV did everything to avoid being a "half-king", Fénelon wanted him to know that "a king does not fulfil the function of a king by looking after the details that those below him could take care of. His essential function is to do what nobody else but he can do. It is to choose carefully those who exercise his authority below him; it is to allocate each the place that suits them best, and to accomplish all in the State, not by himself, which is impossible, but by having everything done by the men he has chosen, whom he trains, whom he corrects. That is the true activity of a king. Have you left all the rest, that which others can manage under you, so that you are able to apply yourself to this essential duty, the one that you alone can fulfil?"* For having dared put this question, Fénelon suffered official disgrace.

Louis XIV had to assume the role of Louis the Great, and nothing must be allowed to harm his grandeur. Madame (Elizabeth Charlotte of the Palatinate, wife of the Duke of Orleans, brother of Louis XIV) was "naively" concerned in 1701 to know "why, in all I these writings, is the king always praised. I was answered that printers had been expressly ordered to print only books that contained a eulogy and this because of the subjects. The French generally read a great deal and because in the provinces they read everything that comes from Paris, praise of the king inspires in them respect and consideration for him."*

Equally, when at court one or another would ask the king a question – hoping for a mission, a grace or a privilege – he would reply with "I shall see". According to Saint-Simon, the king would pronounce this "always with the manner, more or less, of goodwill, almost never with harshness, never with anger." The impatience with which an ageing officer, who had lost an arm in battle, replied to the king was rare enough for Madame to mention it in a letter dated March 17th, 1698. "But sire, if I had replied 'I will see' to my general when he sent me [into battle] on the occasion that I lost my arm, I would still have it and I would not be asking you for something.' That so touched the king that he just as soon granted him a pension."

Thus he imposed his power, one that no-one would question, in a manner that Saint-Simon described as: "Always majestic, although sometimes with gayness, and never before the world [would he leave] anything out of place nor accidental, and everything to the very slightest gesture, walking, his bearing, all about his composure, all is measured, all is decent, noble, grand, majestic and, throughout, very natural."* The diplomat, jurist and theologian Ézéchiel Spanheim reported to his master

Frederick III, Elector of Brandenburg, that the king "has made himself a master of every grace, and thus of everything that has a relationship with the political, military or ecclesiastic state."* Saint-Simon adds: "The respect commanded by his presence, in whichever place he was, imposed silence and even something of fear." Saint-Simon was witness to a scene, in the gardens of Versailles in 1708, when the king erupted in anger. This was because his planned trip to the Château de Marly was thrown into doubt after the Duchess of Burgundy had suffered an injury. Saint-Simon recalls how, after the king's fury: "The event was followed by a silence so complete that one could have heard an ant walking; all dropped their eyes, hardly daring to breath. Everyone was flabbergasted, even the household staff and the gardeners remained still."

VOLTAIRE in *The Age of Louis xiv*, published under the reign of Louis xv, observed that the king "established an order in his house that lasts still now, that regulated ranks and functions." But if Louis xv "joined great politeness to a truly royal attitude", and if "his manner was one of ease and nobility", if he "held his head with much dignity...his manner of look-ing, was imposing but not severe", Madame Campan (who was the appointed reader to the three daughters of Louis xv) observed that it was no longer the manner in which he exercised power that appeared to cap-tivate his entourage. "He was very skilful at doing some futile little things, upon which attention was drawn in the absence of anything else. For example, he was very able to cut off the top of an egg shell with one fell swoop of his fork. He always ate them at his Grand Couvert [large dinner service] and those who came to it on Sundays to view the spectacle returned home less enchanted by the wonderful face of the king than by the talent he showed in opening his eggs."*

IT IS FAR FROM CERTAIN that the skill Louis xv showed in cutting an egg con-vinced his subjects of the strength of his powers. The Cardinal de Bernis was someone who may have been concerned by this. He writes in his

Memoirs of the period in 1757 during which he was for several weeks the first of the king's ministers: "[...] in France the King is not only the master of possessions and life, but also of the spirits of his subjects. What power! And how easy it would be to take advantage."* Does the use of the conditional "it would be" imply that the power of Louis xv is not all it should be? The period of "spirit" at court began with the reign of Louis xv and, noted the Countess of Boigne at the beginning of the 19th Century, "at this time, with spirit, anything went. Spirit played the role that talent is accorded today." It was this "spirit" that had begun putting everything into question.

AT THE BEGINNING of the reign of Louis xiv, the bishop and theologian Jacques-Bénigne Bossuet declared: "Man dies, this much is true; but the King, we say, never dies." Indeed, how many more times would the cry "The King is dead, long live the King!" be called from the balcony of the sovereign's bedchamber? No-one at Versailles took time to reflect upon this warning penned by Fénelon: "When the sovereigns get used to no other laws than their absolute will, they weaken the foundations of their power. There will come a sudden and violent revolution which, far from simply moderating their excessive power, will cut it down to nothing."*

"If, at Versailles today, the noble misery of the warrior succeeds the magnificence of the courts, if canvases depicting miracles and martyrs replace profane paintings, why would the shadow of Louis XIV take offence?"*
Chateaubriand

God? Hero? Emperor?
No…King!

IN 1690 WAS PUBLISHED *THE UNIVERSAL DICTIONARY CONTAINING BROADLY ALL FRENCH WORDS BOTH OLD AND MODERN FRENCH WORDS, & THE TERMS OF ALL THE ARTS AND SCIENCES, RESEARCHED AND COMPILED BY MY LORD ANTOINE FURETIÈRE, ABBOT OF CHALIVOY AND MEMBER OF THE FRENCH ACADEMY.* Under the word 'King', he noted: "One says, also, a king is 'only a king in painting' when he does not govern his State himself, when he leaves the task and the authority to others." As of 1661, Louis XIV set out never to be "a king in painting". However, almost 30 years later at Versailles, where the court had sat for eight years, there was no shortage of paintings of the Sun King. In some he is presented as the god Mars, in others a hero, like Hercules and, elsewhere, dressed in Roman costume, a consul, an emperor. He never ceases to be king. Courtesan and court historian André Félibien wrote to the king, with all necessary elegant deference, about one of his portraits: "Many princes who have worn a crown were only king in appearance. Because the painter was tasked with representing a veritable King, a King, in the body and spirit into which god has poured extraordinary gifts and talents, he had not only to find a way to properly impersonate what we see as so perfect, and so complete in your majestic person, but he has also formed traits and characters which express in diverse ways the beauty and grandeur of your soul."

IT WAS VERY RARE to find any representations that did not scrupulously portray what Félibien called "this grand, noble and natural standing and size which for the Ancients was the stuff of semi-gods."

STRANGELY, in the eyes of the king, an exception to the rule was found in Italian sculptor and architect Gian Lorenzo Bernini, also known as Cavalier Bernin, who Louis XIV invited to create, for the Louvre, the east wing which was to close the Cour Carrée (Square Courtyard). Although the king placed the first stone in one of the projects, he finally renounced the plan. This note by statesman Jean-Baptiste Colbert, minister to the king, may explain why: "The plan by cavalier Benin, although beautiful and noble, was nevertheless so badly thought out for the commodity of the King and his apartment at the Louvre, that with a budget of ten million, he kept him just as tightly in the

Opposite page:
Louis XIV victorious and crowned by Glory, raised stucco by Antoine Coysevox, in the Hall of War.

Opposite page:
Bernini's sculpture
placed at the end
of the Orangery.
Left:
Detail of Louis XIV from
the painting *Decision
taken to make war on
the Dutch, 1671*,
(photo taken during
the restoration work
on the ceiling paintings
of the Hall of Mirrors).

place he was to occupy [there]."* Was that why the king built Versailles? During his stay in Paris, Bernini also sculpted a bust of the king. The 17th Century French fairy tale writer Charles Perrault, in his *Memoirs of My Life*, gives a scathing critique of the work: "The forehead is too hollow, and diminishes something of the king's beautiful facial appearance." He continues: "The nose is a little too tight, and the slash, which arouses so much admiration, is not properly extended. Because it envelopes the end of the king's arm, it can only be a slash that has been placed on his bust, and not the slash that was on the king when his bust was made, because this slash did not surround his arm in the manner that it does."*

CHARLES PERRAULT was the brother of Claude Perrault, who it seems replaced Bernini's project with a colonnade. There was perhaps here a settling of scores in the wings of power. Charles Perrault concludes on the subject of Bernini: "He was a very good sculptor, although he made a quite miserable statue of the king on horseback, which was so little worthy of the prince that the king made him place the head of an ancient upon it. He was a mediocre architect, while having a very high opinion of himself in these matters."* It is not far-fetched to believe that Perrault's opinion moved the king to transform the statue in question into one of Marcus Curtius crossing the flames and to have it placed, so he would rarely see it, at the bottom of the Swiss Pond.

THE STATUE had a long and difficult journey to reach Versailles. When the Marquis de Louvois announced to the king, on November 10th, 1684, that it had arrived at the French Mediterranean port of Toulon, the king replied that it was "quite a good thing that the statue is in Toulon." It did not arrive in the northern port of Le Havre until January 2nd, 1685. From there it was sent by barge down the river Seine to Paris, where it arrived on March 9th. When the king discovered it for the first time upon its arrival at Versailles, his first thought, before giving sculptor François Giradon the task of trans-forming it, was to have it destroyed. Bernini had died on November 28th, 1680, and so never knew the fate of his statue. Judging from this account by Abbot Nicaise, he probably would not have begrudged the king: "I lived with cavalier Bernin before and after his journey to France. He had a great gift for conversation, as much as he had for sculpture, and architecture. He said marvellous things about the king, in all sorts of manners and with reason. He had received such great recompenses that he would have been the most ungrateful of men if he had not told of his thankful-ness. Among other things he said, very agreeably, that the king was the greatest architect of his kingdom."

IN A CONJURING TRICK that history has the knack of, since the Louvre has become the Grand Louvre a copy of this same equestrian sculpture has been placed beside the Pyramid. At the Louvre, where in the end Louis XIV did not want Bernini's project to be the one which sealed the Square Court.

Opposite page:
Bust of Louis XIV,
Gianlorenzo Bernini,
1665.

Precautions to take before entering the stage

WHEN A SIMPLE SUBJECT WISHED ONLY TO APPROACH THE KING, TO SEE HIM, IT WAS SUFFICIENT — IF HE WAS A MAN — TO RENT A HAT AND A SWORD ON THE PLACE D'ARMES.

HOWEVER, IF one wished to be 'presented', that is, with the ambition of being admitted to the court and to live there beside the king, it was very important to be well-prepared. This would be helped by reading from Parisian printer Henri Estienne's book *Two Dialogues of the New Italianized Language,* published in 1579. In it, he gives a seemingly infallible suggestion: "Takes three pounds of impudence, but only the finest, which comes from a rock called the brow of bronze, two pounds of hypocrisy, one pound of dissimilation, three pounds of the science of flattery, two pounds of a nice look; cook it all together in the juice of good favour, during the space of one day and one night, so that the drugs mix well together. Following this, the decoction must be passed through a muslin of broad conscience. Then, when it has cooled, add six spoonfuls of patience water, and three of water of best hopes. There you have a sovereign beverage to become a courtesan, in all perfection and courtisanism [sic]."*

OTHER RECOMMENDED reading (or re-reading) included Fable Three of 17th century French fabulist Jean de la Fontaine's eighth book, *The Lion The Wolf and the Fox*, and to learn by heart the moral of the story: "Beware, ye courtiers, lest ye gain / By slander's arts less power than pain: / For in the world where ye are living / A pardon no-one thinks of giving."

IF ONE DOUBTS ANY of this, one might also refer to this account by courtesans themselves, related by Louis Sébastien Mercier at the beginning of the 1780s: "One must hold the chamber pot for ministers as long as they are in place, and empty it on their heads when they are no longer in place."* It was best to know that courtesans did indeed behave in this manner, and that one is no less at threat by not being a minister. All this

is underlined by the words uttered in 1713 by Marshal de Villars, after his army had done battle with that of Prince Eugene of Savoy. When they met, the marshal said to the prince: "Monsieur, we are hardly enemies; your enemies are in Vienna, and mine in Versailles." And whether one was neither marshal nor minister, the problem remained the same. Every courtesan had enemies, and one's rank at court had little sway in the matter. As La Bruyère put it: "At court one says good things about someone for two reasons; the first is to let him know we are saying good things about him, and the second is so that he says the same about us."*

IT IS THE REASON why Madame de Mamiel hurried to write the following warning to her 18 year-old daughter who, in June 1783, had just taken up her function as lady-in-waiting to Maria-Theresa of Savoy – the wife of the Count of Artois (he who would become Charles X in 1824): "Your fate is in your hands. The merest mistake, the smallest thoughtlessness, can do for you. Danger is under your feet [...] Never travel outside without a

Above:
The Birth at Versailles of the Duke of Brittany, first son of the Duke and Duchess of Burgundy, on June 25th, 1704, 1705.

Below :
"Third Apartment";
Louis XIV playing billiards
with his brother
Philip II of Orleans, the
Duke of Chartres and his
son Louis-Alexandre and
the Count of Toulouse,
among others, Antoine
Trouvain, 1694.

lackey or unless on a sedan chair. Never skimp on your duties towards your adorable mistress [...] and above all be always very prudent. Imagine, my darling daughter, that you will be watched over by everyone, that they will constantly inform themselves about your conduct and that the tiniest fault, however slight that might be, can lose you your station and remove you from the good graces of the princess."*

BETWEEN MAY 6ᵀᴴ, 1682, when Louis XIV surrounded himself at Versailles with the court and government of France, and October 6ᵗʰ, 1789, when Louis XVI left the place for the last time, there was probably only one

courtesan who escaped this rule; the Marquis de Cremeaux d'Entragues, who entered court under Louis XV. A fellow courtesan once asked him what his secret was, to which he answered: "I've always had a principle of never joining in with intrigues, never countering any ambition, of engaging in much coquetry towards men and to be without pretension towards women."*

Above:

Chamberlains preparing the king's table at the court of Louis XIV in Versailles, Antoine Trouvain, 1699.

A PRECIOUS example, and advice.

The Court; a user's guide

A FIRST, ESSENTIAL THING TO UNDERSTAND ABOUT THE COURT IS THAT THERE ARE JUST TWO MAIN COMPONENTS: THE KING...AND ALL THE OTHERS, WHATEVER THESE 'OTHERS' WERE BEFORE ARRIVING. La Bruyère left no ambiguity about this: "One is small within the court. Whatever vanities one may have had, that's the way it is; but evil is common, and even the grand are small." An observation supported by dramatist and moralist Charles Rivière Dufresny: "After the moment these governors, magistrates, warriors and heroes have gloriously made their mark everywhere, they then all come together at the court. Within it, their intrepidness trembles, their pride softens, graveness becomes humanised, and power disappears."* For there is no other power than that of the king.

BRANDENBURG'S SPECIAL ENVOY Ézéchiel Spanheim, author of *Account of the Court of France* in 1690, insists that the king "has made himself a master of every grace, and thus of everything that has a relationship with the political, military or ecclesiastic state; all of which can only contribute to making the court of France most gross."* The reign of Louis xv changed nothing, although he often left Versailles for his other châteaux.

THERE IS THUS the king and the court, and the Abbot of Ailly had no illusions about what the latter is: "The court is the empire of ambition. All other passions, from love, itself, to laws, are subordinate to it. It unites and betrays all." And decade after decade, like reign after reign, nothing changes. Cardinal de Bernis says as much: "One has never been able to count on friendship at the court, but one could count on hate; today, friends are as pale and unfaithful as ever, and enemies are no longer irreconcilable. Relationships change from one day to the other."*

BECAUSE IT IS NECESSARY to constantly beware of the toadying, the flatterers and hypocrites, the sly, the treacherous, the guileful and the pretenders, because one must take note of the denunciations and the

Opposite page:
The balcony of the King's Chamber giving onto the Marble Courtyards, as seen from a door of the apartment of the captain of the guards.

Above:
Louis XIV dubbing the first of the knights of Saint-Louis, May 10th, 1693, François Marot, 1693.

rumours, or what the Countess of Adhémar called "strange prattle", because one must always be aware of the conspiracies, the plots and intrigues, it is also necessary to resign oneself to the fact that one cannot determine the rules of the court. As the dramatist Charles Dufresny wrote: "To make fortune at court, one must be very well-behaved, or completely mad, very modest or very insolent; the first merit everything while gambling nothing. The others manage to pick up something while gambling everything."* La Bruyère offers another description: "Life at the court is a serious, melancholic game which necessitates; organising one's artillery, to have a plan and follow it, parry one's adversary, sometimes take a gamble, and be whimsical. And even after all these dreams and all these measures one can find oneself placed in 'check', and sometimes 'checkmate'. Often, placing one's pawns to best effect, one wins the party; it is the most skilful, or the happiest, who wins the day."* Apparently, the Abbot of Ailly managed to navigate his way through this labyrinth: "To get to the [elevated] situation of dignity [e.g. appointed magistrate] there is what is called the grand route or the beaten track; there is also the back-street, or cross-field path, which is shorter."*

THERE IS BUT ONE RULE that appeared to demand a scrupulous following: one must be noticed by the king. Leaving no doubt about this, Saint-Simon recounted that the king's eyes "cast left and right at his wakening, his retiring, his meals, while passing through his apartments, in the gardens of Versailles where only the courtiers were allowed to follow him. He saw, and remarked upon, everyone. No-one escaped him, including those who hoped not to be seen." Saint-Simon warned of one royal observation that everyone feared: "'He is a man who I never see.' That judgement was irrevocable." La Bruyère added that it was absolutely necessary for every courtesan to know "where he should be best placed to be seen." Nothing changed during the reign of Louis XV. A few days after Robert Damiens attacked the king in the Marble Courtyard, stabbing him with a small-bladed knife, the Cardinal de Bernis,

Below:
*Louis XVI abandons
the rights of the domain
to the laws of the sea in
favour of the inhabitants
of Guyana in 1786,*
René Théodore Berthon,
circa 1817.

who was at Versailles, noted: "Father Desmarets, the King's confessor, saw me as I cut through the crowd to get close to the King's bed. ''Come' he said to me, 'I'll show you a place where, although it's behind everyone, as soon as the curtain is opened, you will be seen by His Majesty.' It seemed to me impossible; he insisted it was so and I let myself be placed there. In the event, I found myself, upon the curtain opening, before the King, who called upon me, from which I concluded that the Confessor knew the optical rules very well."*

THE RAISING OF THE KING'S bed curtain…perhaps the king's confessor knew the rules of theatre better than those of optics. The singularity of Versailles is that it is the only theatre where one enters the stage from both sides of the curtain. It is the only one where the gaze of the king, who has the principal role, decides the fate of he who meets his eyes. This can be condemnation by disgrace, or distinction by grace. And grace, like disgrace, hatches new intrigues. Perhaps alone without illusion, the king knows what's best. *In The Age of Louis xiv*, Voltaire recorded the king's words thus: "Every time I appoint someone to a vacant position, I make one hundred unhappy and one ungrateful." But La Bruyère tells us how these 'unhappy' console themselves: "When someone is placed in a new post, there is an overflow of praise in his favour, which inundates the court and the chapel, which reaches the staircase, the halls, the gallery and all the apartments (…) There are not two contrasting voices speaking about the person; envy and jealousy both speak as adulation."* Yet more theatre.

Opposite page:
The king's bedchamber.

Louis XIV, Philip V

IN HIS *MEMOIRS*, THE MARQUIS DE SOURCHES HAS NO HESITATION IN ASSURING THAT ON NOVEM-
BER **16, 1700:** "IN VERSAILLES THAT DAY TOOK PLACE THE BIGGEST AND MOST EXTRAORDINARY
SCENE THAT EVER OCCURRED IN EUROPE." Colbert's nephew, the Marquis de Torcy,
then Secretary of State for Foreign Affairs, describes here reason for the
event, referring first to the king of Spain: "Charles II, monarch of so many
states, died on the first of November 1700, and soon after his death
caused a general rousing throughout Europe. By his testament, signed
on October 2 previously, he recognised the right of the infant Maria
Theresa, her sister, the Queen of France and mother of the Dauphin, and
that of Queen Anne, her mother, and by consequence the Dauphin, who
was to be the unique heir, according to the laws of the kingdom. But to
avoid the alarm that would be raised in Europe over the union of so many
states with the French monarchy, of which the Dauphin was the only heir
apparent, Charles called to his succession the Duke of Anjou, second son
of the Dauphin, and named him the heir to all his kingdoms and seign-
ories, without exception and without separation."

SEVERAL PAGES of the *Memoirs* of the Duke of Saint-Simon are dedicated to
the surprise and response of Louis XIV and his ministers when they learn
of this testament. At Fontainebleau, the King set about great concentra-
tion on the matter, consulting and meditating, before deciding his action.
What he would announce could only be staged at the theatre of Versailles, to where he returned on Monday, November 15th. "The next day,
on Tuesday November 16th, after his awakening, the King called the Spanish ambassador to his cabinet room, to which Monsieur the Duke of Anjou
had arrived by the rear." The "rear" mentioned here refers to the hidden
stairways and corridors of the palace that, as we have seen, take the
place of stage wings. "The King, indicating [the duke] to him, told [the
ambassador] that he could greet him as his own King. Immediately he
threw himself to the ground, in the manner of the Spanish, and delivered
him a quite long compliment in that language. The King told him [the
ambassador] that he [the duke] did not yet understand the language

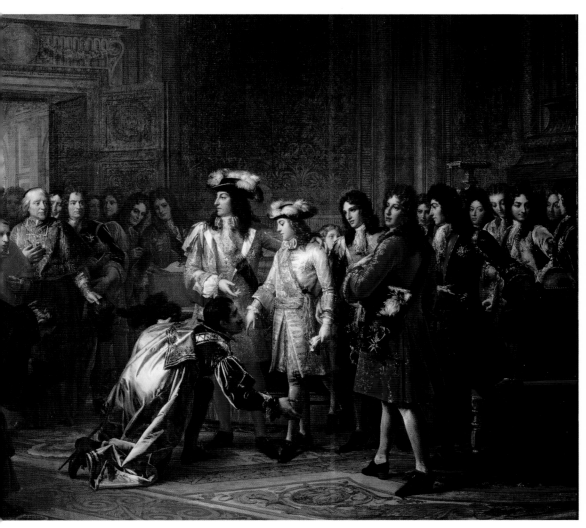

Above:
Proclamation of the Duke of Anjou, King of Spain, as Philip v, on November 16th, 1700,
Baron Gérard, circa 1700.

and that it was for the monarch to reply for his grandson. Immediately afterwards, the King, going against all custom, opened the double inner doors to the cabinet and ordered everyone who was there, almost a crowd, to enter; then, majestically passing his eyes over the large company, he said, while indicating the Duke of Anjou; 'Messieurs, before you is the King of Spain. Birth has called him to this crown, and the dead king by his testament, all the nation had wished it and asked me instantly for it; it was the order of God; I granted it with pleasure.'"*

This next account given by Elizabeth Charlotte, sister-in-law to Louis XIV, in a letter dated November 18th, is notably less pompous: "For your amusement, I am going to tell you how one made the King of Spain. Tuesday morning, the King called the good Duke of Anjou to his cabinet, and told him 'you are the king of Spain.' Just as soon, he had the Spanish Ambassador enter, along with all the Spanish who reside here; they all fell to their knees before their king, kissed his hand one after the other, and placed themselves behind him. Then our King brought the young King of Spain to the salon, where all the court was brought together, and said: 'Messieurs, look here at the King of Spain and salute him.'"*

In all evidence, it is not this laconic account by Madame (the Princess Palatine) which baron Gérard used for a model when he painted the scene on the request of Louis XVIII, who wanted it for his office in the Tuileries. While the Restoration allowed him his nostalgia for that Versailles of the time when he was Count of Provence, during the reign of his brother Louis XVI, it was out of the question that he could be allowed back there. Versailles, once the seat of absolute power, was forbidden to him under the terms of the Charter that saw him take the throne after the abdication of Napoleon 1st in 1814.

Above:
Spain offering its crown to Philip of France, Duke of Anjou,
In the presence of Cardinal Porto-Carrero, November 24th, 1700,
Henri Antoine de Favanne, circa 1704.

The court reduced
to a menagerie

IN THE PREFACE TO HIS *FABLES*, LA FONTAINE HAS THE NEED TO EXPLAIN THAT THEY "ARE ONLY LIGHT-HEARTED IN APPEARANCE, BECAUSE DEEP DOWN THEY CARRY A VERY SOLID MEANING." They are dedicated to "Monseigneur le Dauphin", who thus must know that they "are not only moral tales, they also provide knowledge about other things. The physical properties and characteristics of animals are explained and consequently ours also, because we are a summary of what is good and bad in irrational creatures."* There is therefore no doubt that "these fables are a painting in which each one of us finds himself depicted." Monsieur le Dauphin could not have been better warned that Versailles was a menagerie – if not a jungle.

THE SPECIES within Versailles are distinguished by the very unique criteria of the place. There is one principle that cannot be questioned, and Madame draws attention to this. In a letter dated October 10ᵗʰ, 1693, she wrote: "[...] birth is everything and makes up for any missing qualities." Which does not mean that by being noble one necessarily finds one's place at court. Madame writes in 1702: "Here the lesser nobility is very little considered." This signifies that those who are from the lower nobility can only be despised at court. But they are not the only ones. As La Bruyère put it: "The Grand folk look down upon those of the mind, when they have only the mind; those of the mind look down on the grand ones who have only Grand-ness; the well-bred complain about these and those who have Grand-ness or mind but who are without virtue."*

BEYOND GRANDEUR, beyond intelligence and beyond virtue, there is another criterian that decided the place one has at court; favour. As of 1676, before the court was even installed at Versailles, Madame warned: "This is how things are at court; if the courtesans imagine you are in favour, you can do all that you want, you are certain to be approved; but if they imagine the contrary, they will treat you as ridiculous, even if you descended directly from the sky."* Once the court was enclosed at Versailles, this would become its permanent state. An example was provided in this warning by

the Duke of Guines to his daughters, shortly before they were presented to the court of Louis XVI: "Remember that in this country vice is without consequence, but ridicule kills."

IN "THIS COUNTRY", many would have liked to have known, between 1682 and 1789, what could provoke this fatal ridicule, but never found the answer. One had to resign oneself to the fact that a nothing could provoke it, and this nothing could change from one day to the next. "One sees men fall from great fortune for the same faults that got them there in the first place," wrote La Bruyère, who, with typical cynicism, stressed the word "fault" instead of "quality". He advised: "Do not still hope for candour, frankness, fairness, good offices, services, kindliness, generosity or solidity in a man who has been exposed to the court for any length of time [...]". La Bruyère suggested that just one question was important: "Honour, virtue, conscience are qualities that are always respectable, but often useless; what do you think we can do with a well-meaning man?" The word "man" could just as easily be replaced by "woman". Everyone had to be permanently on their guard.

THE COURT is a theatre of suspicion. That is why one should not believe the Countess of Boigne, who lived within the court of Louis XVI, when she speaks of the existence there of "a palace life where gossip was about the important subjects." It was either an untruth or she forgot to say there was nothing that was important at court. In 1707, Madame caught the true nature of the beast: "What makes us all so serious here are the intrigues; one cannot say a single word without creating an affair." Indeed, she knew this ever since September 1683, just a couple of months after the court settled at Versailles, when she commented: "Here the slightest trifling thing is transformed into a grand affair."

THERE ARE FEW around who criticize the courtesans, and this tiny minority who do attack the court are those more concerned with the conduct of the affairs of the kingdom than of finding favours. They were rewarded with exile or indifference. Fénelon dared to write: "The career of a skilful courtesan loses a State everything. The smallest and most corrupt minds are often those which are best at learning this undignified job." For this Louis XIV sent him off on exile to his bishopric in Cambrai.

LA BRUYÈRE declared: "At the court, a healthy mind tastes solitude and retirement". His views upset many, and the gazette Le Mercure Galant declared that the writer "deserved a place immediately above nothing". Although he succeeded in being elected to the French Academy, when he died during the night of May 10th, 1696, he had no job and was penniless.

IN REALITY, the menagerie that was the court only allowed a choice between two tiresome situations. This is illustrated by the experience of Louis XIV's sister-in-law, Madame, who could not remove herself from the obligations of the court. In 1696 she wrote: "If one does not want to become embroiled in intrigues and gallantries, one must live apart, which is also pretty tiresome." Tiresome if you want to stay, and tiresome if you chose to leave. In 1698 she notes: "Tiresomeness reigns here more than in any other place in the world."

THE PALACE apartments, salons and halls were the wings, the behind-the-scenes of a theatre of hypocrisy. In 1682, the year when the court settled at Versailles, Madame wrote: "[...] since coming here, I have become accustomed to seeing such ugly things that if ever I found myself in a place where falseness did not reign, where lies are not favoured and approved as they are in this court, I would believe I was in paradise."

THE CHOICE BETWEEN paradise and the court appeared to be mirrored in La Fontaine's fable *The Wolf and The Dog*. The tamed Dog tries to convince the wild Wolf what is needed to enjoy his creature comforts: "'To bark a little now and then / To chase off duns and beggar men / To fawn on friends who come or go forth / Your master please, and so forth / For which you have to eat / All sorts of well-cooked meat / Cold pullets, pigeons, savoury messes / Besides unnumber'd fond caresses.'" But, when the Wolf sees marks on the Dog's neck and discovers they are from his chain, he exclaims: "'Chain! Chain you! What! Run you not then / Just where you please and when?' / 'Not always sir, but what of that?' / 'Enough for me to spoil your fat! / It ought to be a precious price / Which could to servile chains entice / For me, I'll shun them while I've wit'." Freedom is of course the price paid by courtesans — but that does not mean that there were no wolves prowling the menagerie of Versailles.

"The King of France is the most powerful prince in Europe. He has no gold mines like his neighbour the King of Spain, but he has greater riches because he finds them in the vanity of his subjects, which is less exhaustible than mines."* Montesquieu

The times of the king

Upon entering the Marble Courtyard one can tell the time by raising one's eyes to the clock that dominates the facing façade, above the balcony and windows of the King's Chamber. The hands of the blue clockface turn from behind a centre featuring the head of Apollo from which rays of the sun indicate each hour. This was far from being the only clock in Versailles. The Count d'Hézecques, who was appointed to the King's Chamber in 1786 at the age of 12, records in *Memories of a Page in the Court of Louis xvi*: "In the Salon of Mercury, we saw a pendulum clock, previously famous. How strange that mechanics have progressed so rapidly. Upon each hour, cocks chanted while rustling their wings, Louis xiv emerged from a temple, and the Renommée (the Renown) came to crown the monarch to the sound of chimes."

The count could have also mentioned another clock, delivered to the palace in 1754, and which was so extraordinary that the hall where it was placed was named the Clock Room. The engineer Claude-Simon Passemant, the clockmaker Louis Dauthiau and the bronze caster Jacques Caffiéri associated their talents to create a mechanical masterpiece capable of giving, as well as the hour time, also the day, the day of the month, the month, the year, the stage of the moon and the movement of planets.

Apart from consulting these fabulous clocks, whoever wanted to find out the time could also have entered the cour des Cerfs (Courtyard of the Stags) and raise their eyes towards a very particular double sundial. Set on the north wall – the instrument must face the south – two discs are placed at the level of the balcony and the cornice. A hole pierced at the centre of each allows a ray of sun that shines through to indicate very precisely upon the engraved stone the time that was that of the Sun King. Some uncharitable minds may see in the courtyard a side to Louis xiv's reign that is other than etiquette, in the wood-mounted hunting trophies of stag's heads that adorned the walls, and which was one of

Above:
The clock in the Marble Courtyard, surrounded by
sculptures of Hercules and Mars in resting position.

romantic adventures. Monsieur de Montespan did not appreciate that his wife became, after Louise de La Vallière, one of the king's mistresses. He was hardly consoled by Molière's verses from *Amphitryon*: "A share with Jupiter / has nothing that in the least dishonours, / for doubtless, it can be but glorious / to find one's self the rival of the sovereign of the Gods."

ANOTHER ALTERNATIVE for timekeeping was simply to follow the king himself. According to Saint-Simon, in his room in the morning, the king "gave each one his order for the day; thus we knew, to within a quarter of an hour, everything that the King had to do." Under the reign of Louis XV, the court could no longer keep time by the king's activities. As was reported in the Journal de Barbier, a chronicle of the Régence and the reign of Louis XV: "The King never spends more than eight consecutive days at Versailles, a fact which causes great problems for all the affairs."

Opposite page
Far left:
One of the sundials
in the Cour des Cerfs.
Right:
The clock of Passemant,
Dauthier et Caffiéri.

"He divided the hours of day and night between his affairs, his pleasures, his devotions and his duties, in such a manner that one learns from courtesans what he is doing and where one can play court to him."* Primi Visconti

The necessity
of splendour

BY THE WILL OF THE KING, VERSAILLES HAD TO BE THE MOST SUMPTUOUS OF ALL PALACES, OF ANY OTHER CHÂTEAU EVER BUILT. In *The Age of Louis XIV,* Voltaire justified "the extreme taste that Louis XIV had for brilliant things". In doing so, he casts aside an accusation levelled against the monarch: "The people believe that a Prince who spends lavishly on buildings and establishments ruins his kingdom; but in fact, he enriches it; he scatters money among an infinite number of artists; all professions benefit from this; industry and circulation increase; the King who allows his subjects to work more is also the one who renders his Kingdom more flourishing."* But the poet Jacques Delille (1738 – 1813), in this stanza from his Gardens, published in 1782, offered a quite different reason for such opulence: "Kings are condemned to magnificence / Those surrounding them expect the efforts of force; / With it hopes of admiration and wonder / Prodigies of luxury and a splendour of arts."*

THIS 'CONDEMNATION' is, of course, the only one that Louis XIV could possibly accept.

THE LUXURIOUSNESS in which Versailles bathed was also its principle reason for being and which ultimately led to its downfall. In 1847, under the reign of Louis-Philippe 1st, King of the French, who chose that the palace be dedicated "to all the glories of France", the French writer Victor Hugo observed: "Luxury is the need of great States and grand civilisations. However, there are times when the people must not observe it. But what is a luxury that cannot be seen? There is a problem here. Magnificence in the shadows, abundance in obscurity, splendour that does not reveal itself, a display that dazzles the eyes of no-one. Is that possible? It is nevertheless something one must consider. When one presents luxuri-ousness to a people during times of scarcity and distress, its spirit, which is one of a child, immediately jumps by a massive degree; they do not think that this luxury provides work, that this luxury is useful to them, that this luxury is necessary. They say to themselves that others

Opposite page:
The trophy of instruments created under Louis XV in the golden cabinet of Madame Adélaïde. The cornice and archivolt in gold and white date from the reign of Louis XIV.

are enjoying it while they are suffering." It was the people of Paris who suffered in 1789, and who came to put an end, in Versailles, to those who were "enjoying it."

THE NOBILITY WERE SWEPT AWAY along with the monarchy. Cardinal de Bernis, who entered the king's Council in 1757 before soon becoming responsible for foreign affairs, said of the aristocracy in his *Memoirs* that "just as riches contribute to power, they are part of the distinction that the nobility have always established among men. Poverty weakens the idea one has of nobility, because apart from diminishing sentiments it also excludes the inseparable idea one has of nobility." Among the crowd which massed in the Marble Courtyard on October 6th, 1789 waiting for the king, or queen, to appear before them on the balcony, who would have known that one century earlier, on May 20th, 1689, Madame, wife of Monsieur, the brother of Louis XIV, wrote in a letter to the Duchess of Hanover: " [...] you cannot imagine in what misery I find myself; I have just one hundred pistoles [gold coins] per month, and I can never give less than one pistole; after eight days, I have nothing left. All my money has gone on fruit, letter carrying and flowers. When the King gives me something, I have to use it to pay off old debts and he only gives it at the New Year. Monsieur gives me not even a single denier. I have to borrow money for the slightest knick-knack." Her misery fell on deaf ears.

BUT IT WAS TOO LATE. What luxuriousness prevailed at Versailles in 1789! In his *Memoirs or recollections and anecdotes*, the Count of Ségur records the state of the court just before the Revolution: "Each one went about eclipsing the others by his luxury, just as conversation was about

Below:
The Council room.

republican matters and a general preaching of equality. There was never at the court [a time of] greater magnificence and vanity, nor less power. The powers of Versailles were lampooned [...] We preferred a word of praise from Alembert or Diderot than the most remarkable favour from a prince. Gallantry, ambition, philosophy, everything was mixed up together and confused; the church dignitaries left their diocese in hope of a ministry; abbots wrote licentious verses and tales."

Below:
Detail of the king's balcony giving onto the Marble Courtyard.

DURING THE REIGNS of Louis XIV and Louis XV, the luxury at Versailles was only briefly interrupted once, in 1709. A hard winter, famine, epidemics and the war had finally had reason of it. On June 8th, 1709, Madame

wrote: "Do you think that we don't hear the lamentations here? Day and night we hear nothing but them! The famine is so violent at present that children devour each other. The King is so decided upon continuing the war, that this morning he sent to the mint his entire gold service, the plates, the platters, the salt pots, in other words anything that contained gold, to produce louis [coins]." Writing during the reign of Louis xv, Voltaire confirmed that the Sun King had "sold four hundred thousand francs -worth of golden tableware; the grandest of noble masters sent the silver tableware to the mint; In Paris, brown bread was the only thing to eat for months. Several families at Versailles, even, nourished themselves on oat bread; Madame de Maintenon gave the example." She did so all the more readily because, ever since she 'reigned' over Louis xv, the court was not what it had been during its first years of existence at the palace. The age of festivities had passed. Already, in 1686, Madame — whose hatred of Madame de Maintenon had never abated — once more wrote to her confidante, the Duchess of Hanover: "In truth, someone who had nothing to do with the court would laugh until tears at the scene of it all. The King believes himself devout because he no longer sleeps with any young woman; all this fear of God consists of being punctilious, to have spies everywhere who falsely accuse people any old how, to flatter his brother's favourites, and to cause torment to people in general. The old girl, la Maintenon, gets pleasure out of making all the members of the royal family appear odious before the King, and to rule over them, except monsieur, who she flatters before the King." More than 20 years later, nothing had changed.

And the "old girl" had lost none of her power.

Appearing and disappearing

THE STAIRCASE OF THE AMBASSADORS THAT LED FROM THE MARBLE COURTYARD TO THE SALONS OF DIANA AND VENUS WAS MORE ELABORATE AND SPLENDID THAN THAT OF ANY OTHER PALACE. It was destroyed in 1752. So if ever you had been hoping, as you mount the stairs designed by architect Ange-Jacques Gabriel to the Salon of Hercules, to walk in the steps of those who have climbed it since the reign of Louis XV, you will be disappointed; the one now in place was in fact completed under the Fifth Republic in 1985. The only staircase existing today upon which all the players of Versailles' history have passed is the Marble Staircase, known as the Staircase of the Queen, built in 1681 in symmetry with that of the Ambassadors. It is, no doubt, to it that the 19th Century French dramatist and poet Alfred de Musset dedicated

Opposite page:
The door leading from
the Cour des Cerfs
to stairways serving
the king's apartments.
Below:
The corridors, doors,
and stairs leading
to the royal apartments.

Above:
A model of the Staircase
of the Ambassadors.
The original was built
between 1674 and 1680
and destroyed in 1752
to enlarge the
apartments.
Following double page:
The Degré du roi Louis xv
staircase (Step of King
Louis xv).

these lines: "Tell us, gracious steps / The kings, princes and prelates / And every hammering marquis / And all the pretty ambitious creatures / For whom you've provided step."* What a shame that the stairs cannot answer, cannot tell us of the very official passages, which were all about appearance. Other stairways served the non-official activities of the palace, such as the 'cupboard staircase', the only one that belonged to the original château built by Louis XIII. This and other hidden steps marked a secret history, one where the nature of the game was to go unseen, or to disappear.

THE STAIRCASE called the Degré du Roi (Step of the King), that leads from the Courtyard of Stags to Louis xv's Small Apartment, was witness to visits of spies and emissaries who had come to report to the king in person. During the reign of Louis XVI, the Count d'Hézecques recorded: "One can compare the palace of Versailles to an enormous labyrinth due to its quantity of halls, corridors, little stairways and apartments that it contains. One needed to have experience of the place to find one's way."

Indeed, Madame de Pompadour's lady-in-waiting, Madame du Hausset, recounted: "One day the King entered Madame's room as she finished dressing; I was alone with her. 'Something very particular has just happened to me', he said; 'Could you believe that entering my bedchamber, having just left my wardrobe, I found a gentleman in front of me?' – 'Oh, God, Sire!' said Madame, aghast. 'It is nothing' he continued, 'but I admit that I had a great surprise. The man appeared quite disconcerted. I asked him – 'What are you doing here' – in a quite polite tone'". The man immediately knelt before the king, to show he was not armed. He was a cook who had taken the wrong staircase. Before long, the guards called by the king confirm the account of the man (who was an expert in preparing the meat dish 'bœuf à l'écarlate'). Again quoting the king, Madame de Hausset continues her account: "'Seeing that this man was so distraught that he could not even find the door, nor stand still, I pulled from my desk fifty louis [gold coins]. 'There, my man, to calm your alarm'. He left after placing himself in a bow.' Madame continued her shocked exclamations over the intrusion into the King's room. He spoke with great clam about this strange appearance, but it was clear he was forcing himself, and that, quite obviously, it had caused him fright."

AND SO IT WAS, throughout the palace, the stairways – so many narrow spirals – appear to pass from one floor to the other, where hidden doors lead to hidden corridors. It was into one of them that Marie-Antoinette, on the morning of October 6th, 1789, fled from her room as the people of Paris climbed the main stairs. To the left of her bed, hidden by a tapestry that covered the wall at the head of it, a door opened into just such a corridor. It led to the King's Apartment, where she found refuge. It was to be the last time that this 'behind the scenes' world of the palace would ever serve the monarchy.

The king and his legacy

LOUIS XIV DIED IN VERSAILLES ON SEPTEMBER 1ST, 1715. The Duke of Orleans, who had become the regent, had no desire to remain in the palace to govern. On September 9th, he took the then-five year-old Louis XV to Paris. His education would be performed at the Tuileries and at Vincennes. The palace and the town emptied. The king's majority should only be proclaimed upon his 13th birthday, on February 23rd, 1723. But despite that, the court returned to Versailles on June 15th, 1722, probably because Cardinal Dubois, furious that he had not yet become prime minister, did everything he could to convince the Regent to make the move. That day a carriage pulled up and out stepped Louis XV, the regent and his son, the Duke of Chartres, the Duke of Bourbon, Marshal Villeroi and the bishop of Fréjus, who had overseen the king's education. After a prayer in the chapel, the 12 year-old Louis XV led those accompanying him into the palace gardens. During two hours, he ran along the alleyways, up and down the steps, flitting from fountain to pond. When he returned to the palace, he lay down on the floor inside the Hall of Mirrors.

IMAGINE HIM, stretched out on his back in the centre of the hall. Imagine his eyes gazing over the Le Brun's ceiling, and the words; 'The King governs by himself'. The gazette *Le Mercure Galant* reported in January, 1685, that the original inscriptions in Latin had been replaced by words in French. But the king considered that those conceived by the Academy member François Charpentier – THE KING HIMSELF TAKES OVER THE MANAGEMENT OF STATES, AND GIVES HIMSELF ENTIRELY TO THE AFFAIRS M DC LXI – were too pompous, and had Racine and Boileau replace them. It is their text that Louis XV, lying on his back, can read. Alas, Monsieur Pignol de la Force is not at his side to explain the allegories which surround his great-grandfather. He could have found illumination from one of the four first editions of *'New Descriptions of the Palaces and Arches of Versailles and Marly'*, available from The Widow of Florentin Delaulne, rue Saint Jacques, which contained, according to its title: *'a historical explanation of all the Paintings, Canvases, statues, vases and Ornaments that can be seen there; their dimensions,*

Opposite page:
The absolute power of the monarch, ceiling painting in the Hall of Mirrors completed between 1679 and 1684 by Charles Le Brun,

LE ROY
GOVVERNE
PAR LVI MÊME

and the names of the painters, sculptors and engravers who made them, enriched by several line-engraved illustrations.'

INSIDE IT, the young Louis XV could have read: 'This Prince is represented here in the flower of his youth on a throne, having the right hand on a boat's tiller. The Graces are standing close to him, and Tranquillity in the form of a seated woman, holds a pomegranate, the symbol of the union of peoples under the sovereign's authority. France is also seated, crushing Discord under the weight of the shield upon which it is leaning. Hymenaios lights the scene with her torch and signifies continuing marriage rejoicings. The flowers and fruit that tumble from the urn of the Seine marks the fertility of the country it waters. The bottom of the painting is filled with naked children, who represent, by their different attitudes, the festivities and pleasures that one enjoys in a young court full of politeness and brilliance. The Monarch is solely preoccupied by the Glory that presents itself to him, and which causes to shine to his eyes a crown enriched with stars. Minerva is beside the throne and Mars is above it. Time lifts one of the corners of the Pavilion and reveals the wonderful actions of the King. The Divinities; Jupiter, Juno, Neptune, Vulcan, Pluto, Hercules, Diana and Ceres are attentive and look down over the monarch from the sky above. The sun, upon its chariot, rushes to witness the scene, and Mercury flies to announce his glory to all the Earth."*

"When he must threaten,
he has lightening in his hands.
Every king, without elevating himself above humans,
Can against criminals throw thunder;
But when he makes people happy, he is god on earth.'
Jean-Jacques Rousseau

Left:
*Louis XV, King of France,
sitting in his grand
gown, aged five years,*
Hyacinthe Rigaud,
circa 1715-1716.

To what glory should he be thinking about, this young king lying on his back and who his subjects call 'le Bien Aimé' ('the Well-Loved')? Perhaps, shortly beforehand, he had been read the following words, written in 1700 by Louis XIV for his grandson who had become Philip V, King of Spain: "I finish by giving one of the most important pieces of advice I can. Do not let yourself be governed; be the master; never have a favourite or a prime minister. Listen, consult your advisor, but decide. God, who has made you King, will give you the light that you need, as long as your intentions are good ones." Could Louis XV, aged just 12 years, have understood these intentions?

The Hall of Mirrors

IN A LETTER DATED APRIL 15TH, 1685, MADAME DE SÉVIGNÉ WROTE: "NOTHING EQUALS THE BEAUTY OF THIS HALL IN VERSAILLES. This sort of royal beauty is unique in the world." It was the architect Jules Hardouin-Mansart who was given the task of transforming into a hall the terrace that once gave out onto the gardens. It was down to him to make a palace of a castle, and one all the more incomparable because it was to be the residence of the greatest king of the universe. The hall was completed in 1684. As of January 12th, 1685, it provided the most dazzling manner with which to show Europe the power of Louis XIV. That day, the sovereign was host to the doge of Genoa. The gazette *Le Mercure Galant* reported the event, recording that the Marshal de Duras escorted the doge "all the way to the foot of the throne of His Majesty. It was in silver and raised by just two steps. The Dauphin and [the king's brother] Monsieur were at the sides of the King, and His Majesty was surrounded by all the blood princes and by his grand officers of close rank to him in such ceremonies."*

BECAUSE THE REPUBLIC of Genoa had the impudence of building galleys for Spain, the king had ordered the town's bombardment the previous year, between May 17th and 22nd. Europe could only be astonished at the very presence of the doge that day in the hall, for the constitution of Genoa decreed that a doge who leaves his town will be stripped of his function. According to Voltaire's *The Age of Louis XIV*, the Marquis de Seignelai asked the doge what he found most remarkable in Versailles: "Finding myself here," was his answer. The proof this relayed to Europe of the king's power, and that of Versailles, was such that the doge was the first 'prince' of Europe to be received in the Hall of Mirrors, and the last. The king could be certain that the ambassadors would report back to their masters on the event, with a description of such magnificence that none would want to measure themselves against it. To have any such intention would run the risk of depleting one's own power. On September 1st, 1686, Louis XIV granted an audience in the hall for the ambassadors of the King of Siam, Phra Naraï, and another, on February 19th, 1715, for the Persian ambassador. In 1686, the Duke of Aumont, Chief Gentleman

Opposite page:
View of the Hall
of Mirrors, seen from
the Hall of War.

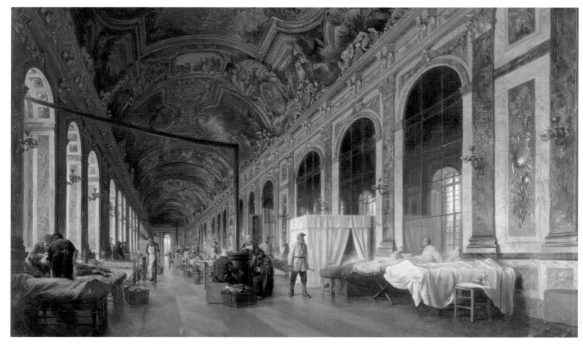

Above:
The Grand Hall of Versailles, 1750.

Page 102, top:
Reparation for Louis XIV from the doge de Genoa, Francesco Maria Imperiale-Lercari, in the Grand Hall of the palace of Versailles on May 15th,1685, Claude-Guy Hallé.
Bottom: *An episode of the 1870 war.* The Prussian wounded receive treatment in the Hall of Mirrors of the palace of Versailles, Victor Bachereau-Reverchon.

Page 103, top:
January 18th, 1871: Wilhelm 1st of Prussia is proclaimed Emperor of Germany in the Hall of Mirrors in Versailles, Anton von Werner, 1885.

Bottom:
Signature of the treaty of Versailles, June 28th, 1919, William Orpen, circa 1925.

Page 104-105:
The Hall of Mirrors.

Above:
The masked ball for the marriage of Louis, Dauphin of France, with Maria Theresa of Spain in Versailles in February 1745, in the Hall of Mirrors, Charles Nicolas le Jeune Cochin, 1745.

"It is this beautiful hall that I call a luminous alley, because it is lighted as if the sun itself was the light, because it has mirror perspectives that double its length, orange trees in great silver tubs, and one can stroll there without becoming hot, as if one was in the shade…"* Mademoiselle de Scudéry

of the Chamber, took measures to "allow that six people can pass forwards in the empty space in the middle of the hall." However, the *Mercure Galant* reported that in 1715 "the crowd of courtesans was so large that, despite the vast stretch of the hall, the Ambassador spent some time unable to approach the throne."

THIS HALL, whose original dimensions were 40 toises (a measurement equalling six feet) long and 36 feet wide (or: 77.7 metres by 11.66 metres), never ceased to be a theatre of history. On December 7th, 1697, it was where the Duke of Burgundy, Louis XIV's grandson, married 12 year-old Marie-Adélaïde of Savoy. On February 25th, 1745, a masked ball was held there to celebrate the marriage of the dauphin with Maria Theresa Antonia Rafaela, Infant of Spain. The king himself is there, or could have been there – the doubts of a masked ball are such – disguised as a yew tree. It was a sumptuous spectacle, which left the *Mercure Galant* envoy lost for words: "I will not even try to describe the richness and diversity of the costumes. It would suffice to tell you that imagination could go no further."

CENTURIES PASS, and with them regimes. After the fall of the Second Empire, the Hall of mirrors became a hospital for Prussian soldiers. Windows were pierced to accommodate the pipes of the stove heaters. On January 18th, 1871, Wilhelm 1st became Emperor of Germany there. To wash away the effrontery, it was there, 48 years later on June 28th, 1919, that France demanded that the allies and the defeated German Empire signed the Versailles peace treaty that ended the First World War. It was also there where, in 1938 on the eve of the Second World War, then-French President Albert Lebrun held a dinner in honour of British king George VI. Between June 4th and 6th, 1982, it was there that François Mitterrand, France's Socialist president elected one year earlier, hosted the first G7 meeting on French soil, demonstrating to his guests, including US President Ronald Reagan and UK Prime Minister Margaret Thatcher, that the left-wing French government could turn on the style.

Opposite page:
Hall of Mirrors as seen from the Hall of War .

Etiquette, rank, positions and roles...

WHOSOEVER ENTERS VERSAILLES SHOULD KNOW THAT THE SLIGHTEST GESTURE IS ALSO A SIGN. One had to be perfectly initiated to the meaning of these signs, and vigilance was required to avoid a blunder. To be a courtesan implies a scrupulous knowledge of the requirements of etiquette. It is, behind the scenes, equivalent to a *deus ex machina*. Etiquette is prevailed upon to organise and rule the life at the court, right down to the smallest details. To be convinced of the consequences of a tiny mistake, a mere triviality, within a court where everything is commented upon, one has only to read Saint-Simon's description of the king's greetings: "Towards women he plainly removed his hat, but from a certain distance; towards titled people he would hold it in the air, or to his ear, for a few notable moments; towards the true gentry, he would place his hand on his hat. For blood princes he lifted it as he would for women. If he approached ladies, he would only cover his head again when he had left them." Here were the signs, or not, of a sovereign's interested attention, or perhaps the chance to obtain favour.

FOR MORE THAN A CENTURY, whoever lived at Versailles knew that etiquette had to be followed exactly. All the more so because it governed titles, and thus language, as much as gestures. Its complexity was such that Madame, to dispel a very unacceptable misunderstanding, was moved to write in 1707 to one of her relatives: "I see that you take my son for a blood prince. But he is not one. His rank is one of a grandson of France; this is superior to that of blood princes, and has more privileges. The grandsons of France greet queens, sit down before them, mount in their carriages; blood princes can do none of these things. Their domestic staff has certain exemptions and serve to the rules of ascendancy. They have a first horseman, a first butler. Blood princes have none of all that, nor do they have a body guard, like my son, nor Swiss guards."*

Opposite page:
The alter and organ of
the Saint-Louis chapel.

DURING THE REIGN of her father Louis xv, Madame Adélaïde would be furious to hear herself called 'Royal Highness'. Birth did not decide title. It was

Above:
The presentation of the order of the Holy Spirit in the chapel of Versailles, Nicolas Lancret, 1724.

therefore important to ensure one was aware of all the slightest changes that may occur. Thus, shortly after the death of the great dauphin, Madame had to swiftly inform the Duchess of Hanover of the manner in which he who was until then Duke of Burgundy must now be addressed. "I have been told this instant on what footing the new dauphin (ex-Duke of Burgundy) will be. He will not simply carry the title Monsieur, like his father. While speaking to him, one will call him only Monsieur; on speaking of him, one will refer to him as *Monsieur le dauphin*, but on writing to him one must address him as *Monseigneur*."

OF COURSE, these decisive nuances are also applicable in the chapel, as Madame makes clear in 1710: "You must bear in mind that here, at the mass, we follow distinctions by rank. It is thus that no-one other than the granddaughters of France can have a Chapel Clerk who gives the response of mass and holds a candle from the *Sanctus* of the Preface until the *Domine, non sum dignus*. The blood princesses are allowed neither the candle nor their own Chapel Clerk and it is their pages who utter the response to the mass. At the end of mass, the priest brings the Corporal to be kissed; it goes no further than the children of France. It is the same for a chalice from which is offered wine and water; we alone have right to this, and it does not reach the blood princes. You see then that here there are ceremonies as much as there is devotion." The explanation of the place that these ceremonies hold even within church is summed up in one phrase: "In everything spiritual, we always have, in this country, consideration of the worldly matters."

IF ETIQUETTE is imposed inside the palace chapel, how could it escape the interior of a carriage? The Duke of Luynes was no doubt aghast to have had to note, on October 10th, 1736, that: "Mme de Boufflers always follows Mlle de Clermont; she was at the front in the Queen's carriage, and Mme de Boufflers at the back. All that is against the rules and customs. Mme de Boufflers should have been at the back of the carriage with Mlle de

Clermont to her left; she should have always walked on the left of Mlle de Clermont, pass through the doors at the same time as her, with the simple difference that is that the princess should have the shoulder ahead of that of the duchess who accompanies her." The duke was saddened to learn that the queen, Maria Leszczynska, did herself decide to end with the requirement that Monsieur le Dauphin, Madame la Dauphine and Mesdames kiss her hand each time they meet her. "[…] she told them not to kiss her hand except for the first and last time they meet her in the day. A number of people think the queen was wrong to end a custom that maintains respect and endearing."

THERE WERE OTHER changes made during the reign of Louis XIV, in particular concerning the entrances before the king. In January, 1749, the Duke of Luynes sadly observed: "No-one enters the œil-de-bœuf while in waiting anymore; the door is only opened to each one at the moment he is to meet the King. This arrangement has caused much sorrow for the courtesans who have no invitation, according to what I have heard; all the more so because once inside the œil-de-bœuf they are still some considerable distance from the King, who for some time now no longer sleeps in the adjoining bedchamber, but rather in the chamber he had made in the place where there was previously a billiard." Already, 10 years prior to this, the king broke the most sacred rules of etiquette. It was well-known that the monarch was expected, every Holy Saturday, "to touch" those who were ill. But that year, according to the *Journal de Barbier chronicle of the Régence and the reign of Louis XV*, "with the pretext of some sort of incommodity, he held neither his ceremony nor his Easter; this caused great scandal at Versailles."

AT THE END OF LOUIS XIV'S REIGN, in 1711, Madame wrote: "There is no slavery comparable to the subjugation in which the King holds his family." The etiquette he imposed regulated a performance to which, reign after reign, the leading roles were as subordinate as the extras. The Duke of Luynes, writing while Louis xv was king, noted: "Because M. de Chatillon was absent, the officiers du gobelet (equivalent to royal sommeliers) advanced that it was they who should provide Monsieur le Dauphin with what to drink, instead of the vice-governor. They were sanctioned for their supposition." He did not mention that during the contention between the sommeliers and the vice-governor, the dauphin was thirsty! Simil-arly, one winter's night during the reign of Louis xvi, Marie-Antoi-nette was shivering from cold in her bedchamber. It so happened that that evening her shirt gown should have passed from her first chamber maid to a lady-in-waiting who is present and who, because the Duchess of Orleans then entered the Queen's Bedchamber, must return the shirt gown to the first chamber maid who is the only one between them who can permit herself to hand it to the duchess who, when the Countess of Provence, the queen's sister-in-law, suddenly joined everyone in the room, is the only person who is allowed to dress the queen. And when the duchess at last passed the gown upon the queen, upsetting her hair, the latter growls: "How despicable! How importunate!"

YET MORE IMPORTUNATE was that the queen had to give birth in public. A wit-ness described the scene in her room on December 19th, 1778, when Marie-Antoinette was to give birth for the first time: "During the night the

"Reason is a historian, but passions are actors."* Comte Antoine de Rivarol

Above:

The birth of the Duke of Burgundy, grandson of Louis XV, 1751.

King took the precaution of having the huge partitions [folding screens] surrounding Her Majesty's bed attached by cords. Without this foresight, they would undoubtedly have been toppled upon her. It became impossible to move in the chamber, which was filled with such a mixed crowd, that one could imagine one's self in a public square. Two Savoyards climbed upon the furniture to see, at their ease, the queen who was placed in front of the chimney, upon a bed dressed for the occasion." The public childbirth is a ritual which the monarchy would never question; it was important, especially if the new-born was the dauphin, that no-one could question the baby had been substituted for another. That day, Marie-Antoinette brought to the world Marie-Thérèse Charlotte of France, Madame Royale. She would become the only member of the royal household to survive the Revolution when, on her 17th birthday, her captivity was ended in an exchange of prisoners.

"Nothing bores and tires me as much as this artificial activity, this idle occupation, this importance given to the puerile things which make up the life of a courtesan."*
Countess of Boigne

IF FOR HER MOTHER, Marie-Antoinette, the etiquette that delayed the arrival of the shirt gown was importunate, it also provided a distraction for her father, Louis XVI in an incident recalled by the Countess of Boigne: "The first chamber valet gave the shirt to the person most qualified, the blood princes if they were present. This is a right, and not a favour. When it concerned a person he was familiar with [present in the bedchamber], the King often carried on with little tricks to put it on, avoiding the other, walking past him, having himself pursued and joining hearty laughter to all this charming joking, which caused suffering to those who were sincerely attached to him." Madame Royale, when she became Madame la Dauphine under the Restoration, tried in vain to revive the etiquette. That was when the Countess of Boigne observed, without regret: "But it could never take hold again..." The great age of etiquette was limited to that of Versailles.

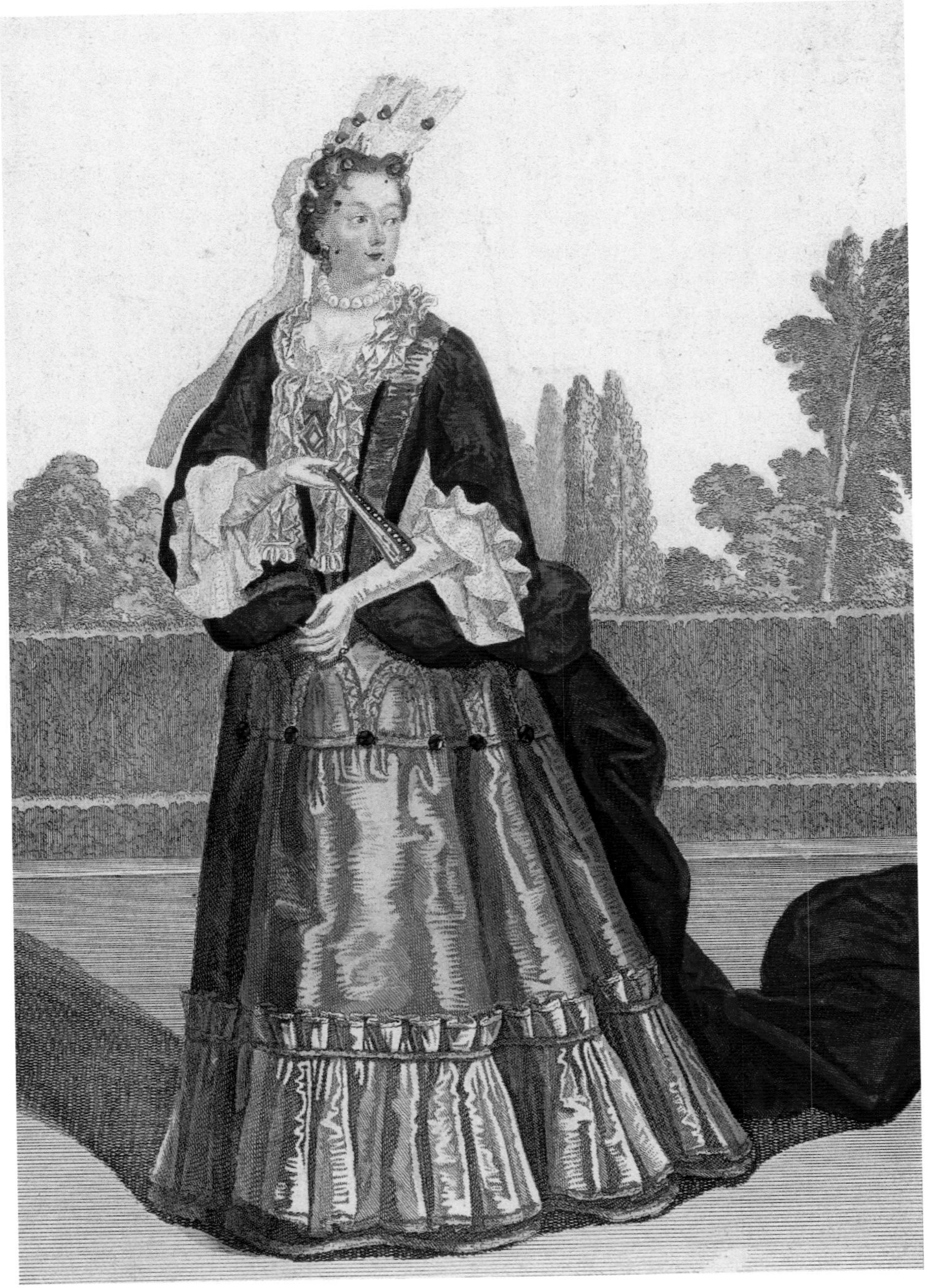

The rule of fashion

HISTORY BOOKS DO NOT REVEAL EVERYTHING WHEN THEY STATE THAT LOUIS XIV, LOUIS XV AND LOUIS XVI WERE THE ONLY MONARCHS TO REIGN FROM VERSAILLES; BECAUSE BEHIND THE REIGNS OF ALL THREE KINGS THERE WAS ALSO THE RULE OF FASHION. Between May, 1682, and October 1789, no-one could have the temerity to contradict the Count of Ségur when he wrote: "At the court as in Paris, everything is subordinated to fashion; this mad power briefly raises or lowers the value of each individual, not according to merit but by the slightest consequence that attracts or repulses attention towards him."

FASHION, of course, concerns hairstyles. The following is Madame's exclamation shortly before the court settled at Versailles: "No-one, in all France, excepting those who always wear old-fashioned things, has any other kind of hairstyle. How you would laugh if you saw me with these turkey tufts!" These 'tufts', as is the nature of fashion, did not last. On January 14th, 1988, Madame insisted: "In court nobody wears headscarves any more, but hairstyles are getting higher and higher by the day." Fashion also concerns make-up. The Scottish author and poet Tobias George Smollett, briefly present at the court in 1760s, expressed surprise at the women who apply to their faces so much white and red make-up. In *his Travels Through France and Italy* he recounts that the make-up, or fard, "not only destroys all distinction of features" but rendered their appearance alarming or, in the best of cases "inspires nothing but ideas of disgust and aversion." Furthermore, "without this horrible masque, no married lady is admitted at court or in any polite assembly." The French philosopher and social commentator Montesquieu was no less surprised by the powers of fashion, and its changing nature: "One can sometimes see on faces a prodigious quantity of specks and they all disappear the next day." He is even more astonished at the consequences all this has: "Who could believe it? Architects often have to heighten, drop or widen doors according to what is demanded by women's costumes, and the rules of their trade serve these whims."

Opposite page:
Anne-Louise-Bénédicte de Bourbon, Duchess of the Maine.

FASHION was everywhere: On March 3rd, 1695, Madame observed: "No-one here wants to dance anymore. On, the other hand, they are all taking music lessons. It is the great fashion now and it's followed by all the young people of quality, men as much as women."

TWO YEARS LATER, fashion had even reached affairs of the heart: "Love in marriage is no longer fashionable at all. Spouses who love each other are thought of as ridiculous." Soon, in the streets they were singing: "It's no longer fashion at court / to have an intrigue of the heart / The King no longer tries to please / Laire, lalaire, lonlaire, lalaire, lonla."

THIS REIGN OF FASHION at Versailles is in no way a coup d'état; if it offers no threat to the power of the king this is because the monarch has himself invited fashion to take on an importance that serves him well. It was only too rare to hear any criticism of it, such as this observation from Fénelon in a letter to Louis XIV: Have you taken the care to repress luxury and to stop the ruinous inconsistency of the fashions? [...] Have you not yourself contributed to such a great evil by an excessive magnificence?"

BUT THE SUN KING could not have cared less about Fénelon's bitter words, for fashion served him even beyond his kingdom. While its powers spread across Europe, it also reinforced those of the king. Madame, writing about the rising height of hairstyles, commented: "The King at table today said that a man called d'Allart, a hairdresser by trade, had styled the hair of ladies in England so high that they could no longer sit in their sedan chairs; and that over there, all the ladies, in order to follow French fashion, have raised the height of their chairs [carriages]." If the king took the time to engage in such banter, it indicated that such matters were not entirely futile. Some 80 years later, Smollett, in his *Travels Through France and Italy*, scornfully wrote that "France is the general reservoir from which all the absurdities of false taste, luxury, and extravagance have overflowed the different kingdoms and states of Europe." The fashion imposed at Versailles by Louis XIV may have been, after all, his greatest victory, for it had invaded all of Europe.

Below:
*Elisabeth-Charlotte de
Bourbon, Mademoiselle
de Chartres.*

Below:
*Marie-Olympe
de la Porte-Mazarin,
Marquise
de Belfonds.*

Above:
Toilet cabinet in the apartments
of Marie-Antoinette.

Closet drama

IN A LETTER WRITTEN ON FEBRUARY 12, 1683, MADAME THE MARQUISE DE SÉVIGNÉ WAS DELIGHTED: "I've just returned from Versailles. I saw such beautiful apartments. I am charmed by them. If I had read about them in whatever novel, I could only have dreamt of seeing them for real. I saw and touched them: it is enchanting. It is a true liberty, it is no illusion, everything is magnificent." Many years later, in 1774, the German court painter (and later architect) Johann Christian von Mannlich, employed in the services of Christian IV, Duke of Zweibrücken, visited Versailles. It was the end of Louis XV's reign, and the beginning of that of Louis XVI. Von Mannlich described the palace as "a monument to ego, rather than that of good taste" although he admired "the magnificence of the interior." Thus it appears that Louis XIV, in creating Versailles, had definitively changed the order of things

THE COUNT OF BUSSY-RABUTIN despite being jailed in the Bastille when he was not exiled to his property, recognised in his *Memoirs* that: "The King is clean and magnificent regarding his dress, his furniture, his tables, his hair, his grand style, his buildings; in everything, finally. The royal households, which before him were, under an air of grandeur, the most unclean in the world, now have the magnificence of kings, and the cleanliness of private houses."* That is not the opinion of Louis XIV's sister-in-law. Madame, Princess Palatine, noted: "The King and Monsieur were used to the dirtiness inside the households ever since childhood, so much so that they did not think things could be any different; that said, they were very clean about their person." It is thus that the only odour that discomforted the king was that which was the object of a letter to the Marquis de Louvois, dated November 9th, 1684: "Remember to look after my room where the odour of gold colour [paint] is very nasty." As of the following day, recorded Louvois, efforts were made to "get lots of fires burning there, and from time to time the opening of windows, so as to pass off the bad odour."

Above:
The bath in
the apartments
of Marie-Antoinette.

Among the some 200 apartments that the palace contains, there was at least one which bathed in odours that were hardly those of gold but rather "the latest miseries that mother nature has chosen to inflict upon us" according to the report by the inspectors of the King's Buildings. The inspectors had been summoned after one of the apartments had just been attributed, and found that "the bedroom is infected by the areas surrounding the common amenities [i.e. toilette area] that are in an adjacent corridor; gaps in the walls allow the odour to sweep into this room, making it uninhabitable."*

If Versailles was splendour and magnificence, one could also find there, as Voltaire recorded after his own personal experience, more than one "shitty hole". Indeed, more still, as Madame, Princess Palat-ine, wrote: "It is impossible to leave one's apartment without seeing someone pissing." The fitting of 'closets for affairs' ('cabinet d'affaires'), or what were also called 'comfort closets', had been continually postponed. During the reign of Louis XVI, one of the palace intendants wrote: "I see this establishment [of closets] as being absolutely indispensable, given the enormous quantity of persons who do not know where to go to do their needs and who go about doing them in the corridors, in the halls that are now closed, or exposed in the park." If the expense for their installation was agreed, they were never built. One had to know what one was up against when navigating Versailles 'behind-the-scenes'.

Below:
Between the library and
the 'comfort' closet there
is but one step...

Left:
*View of the Royal Courtyard
of the Château de Versailles,*
Israël Silvestre, 1685.

Louis XIV's hairshirt

OF THE MANY THINGS THAT DETERMINED THE CHOICE OF VERSAILLES FOR LOUIS XIV, LOVE WAS ONE OF THE MOST IMPORTANT. The Duke of Saint-Simon explained: "The love for Mme de la Vallière, which was first a mystery, gave rise to frequent promenades at Versailles, which was then a little castle of cards built by Louis XIII who was fed up, and his entourage even more so, with having to often sleep in a nasty wagoner's tavern and in a windmill [...]." Ézéchiel Spanheim, special envoy to the court of Brandenburg, who arrived in France in 1680, confirmed as much: "This tender and reciprocal love, however little legitimate, accompanied by all the attentions that it could inspire for two passionate lovers, gave first place to the retreats to Versailles, and afterwards to entertainment and scenes of gallantry to flatter the passion of a King [and] lover."

THIS VERSAILLES that Louis XIV chose against the Louvre and the Saint-Germain châteaux was "the most sad and unprepossessing of all places, without a view, with no woods, no water, no land, because all was quicksand and marshland, and by consequence without any air, which could not be good," wrote Saint-Simon. In *The Age of Louis XIV*, Voltaire commented: "The nation desired that Louis XIV prefer his Louvre and his capital to Versailles, which the Duke of Créqui described as a favourite without merit."* But nothing would dissuade the king. "He was happy to tyrannise nature, to tame it with the force of art and treasures." This was not an easy task, above all because the king refused to admit that it was necessary to demolish the castle built by his father. The writer Charles Perrault reported that the sovereign, "stirred by anger," announced to Colbert and those in his entourage: "Do what pleases you, but if you knock it down, I will have it rebuilt just as it is and without changing anything." The Marquis de Sourches noted, on September 23rd, 1687: "[...] basically, whatever the ills of Fontainebleau, the air was always better than that of Versailles, where it was always very bad; but in particular that year, it seemed to be infested, there being up to twelve hundred taken ill among the two battalions of the King's regiment who camped

Opposite page:
Portrait of Madame de Maintenon, French School, 1680.

there to carry out the work. There were also more than twenty thousand sick among the thirty-six battalions working at the river Eure, and which made the King, despite his eagerness to advance with the work, decide to send them back to their barracks on October 1st, and then the continual downpour of rain that occurred at the time brought forward their departure."

JUDGING BY the *Memoirs* of the Duke of Saint-Simon, and others again, nature took its revenge. The duke makes the disenchanted observation that the king, at Versailles, "built one after the other, without a general plan, beauty and ugliness stitched together, the vast with the cramped." The king is no better off than anyone else: "His apartment and that of the Queen had the worst of inconveniences, with the view of closets and all that is most obscure behind, the most confined, the most stinking." Under the reign of Louis XVI, there were still complaints about these "apartments with which the palace was doted [which] were too incommodious for persons well-established at Versailles." On this note, Mademoiselle de Montpensier never forgot what were at first her own quarters: "Upon arriving at Versailles, I was put in a new apartment which was the most beautiful in the world. All the windows were open. When I returned to it in the evening, there was a strong and large presence of smoke, which prevented one from smelling the paint; but when I had gone to bed, this odour came over me so violently that I could not sleep. I got up at daybreak and left for Paris."

EVEN IF ONE DISTANCED oneself from the palace itself, it made little difference. "From the gardens, one enjoyed the beauty of the entire ensemble, but it was like looking at a palace that had been burnt, where the last floor and the roofs were still missing." There could only be resignation to the fact that the vast building site that was Versailles would never be completed. In 1715, Saint-Simon observed: "There will never be an end to the monstrous defects of a palace so immensely expensive, with its accompaniments that are even more so: the orangery, vegetable gardens, kennels, the Great and Small Stables the same, what prodigious dependencies. In the end, it has not been possible to finish this Versailles of Louis XIV, this so-ruinous and so distasteful masterpiece, where the changes to the water basins and copses have buried more gold than it would seem likely. Among all the salons heaped one upon the other, there is no hall for comedies, nor banquet hall, nor ballroom, and in front and behind there is still much to be done." *

LOUIS XIV was no doubt the first convinced of the problem. In one of her letters dated November 5th, 1699, Madame recounts a rare "admission" by the king. "The King admits himself that there were defects in the architecture of Versailles. This springs from the fact that, in principle, he did not want to build such a vast palace, but rather to simply enlarge a small castle that was found there. Following that, the place pleased the King; but he could not reside there, given the insufficiencies of the lodgings. So, instead of entirely demolishing the small château and building a large one upon a new design, and to save the old château, he had constructions raised all around, covering, as it were, with a beautiful coat, and that ruined everything."

IT COULD BE suggested that Versailles was something of a hairshirt for Louis XIV. It was after all where the court was invited to join the king only in 1682; where some few months after the death of queen Maria Theresa of Austria on July 30th 1683, the king married Madame de Maintenon, during the night of October 9th; which was also a place Louis chose through love for Louise de la Vallière whom he made duchess in 1667. It was perhaps, also, the cilice of penitence for a king driven to repentance and devotion by the Marquise de Maintenon who, while becoming a waiting maid for the dauphiness in 1680, was the only woman to have lived at Versailles throughout the reign of Louis XIV.

Left:
*The Grand and Small
Stables as seen from the
Palace,* Jean-Baptiste
Martin, circa 1690.

For the love of the king

During Louis xiv's reign, Fénelon raged that "this large number of women who freely go about the court is a monstrous abuse to which the nation has bee accustomed." But his ire had no effect. Women, such as Madame de La Vallière, were one of the very reasons for the existence of Versailles, just as they were also, like Queen Marie-Antoinette, one of the reasons for its fall. One after the other – queens, mistresses and courtesans – they never ceased to play an essential role at the court. The kings were continuously ruled by some of them. During the reign of Louis xv, it was a subject that sparked the fury of the Marquis d'Argenson, who noted in his *Journal* on September 20th, 1752: "The Countess of Toulouse has taken on a great ascendancy over the king; his majesty never stops chatting with this princess, when she is with him. It raises the credit of the Noailles, who were already only too harmful for the affairs of the kingdom. All this is becoming more than ever the government of inner circles, of women and of eunuchs, and their pettifogging passions. There you have the result of our monarchs' residence in Versailles."

The jealousies and hate that were provoked there, year after year, saw strings of venomous intrigues and the pitiless settling of scores amid torrents of spiteful words. It was thus that Madame du Hausset lent these following words to Madame de Montespan when the latter was the king's mistress: "He does not love me, but he feels he owes it to his subjects and to his own grandeur to have the most beautiful mistress in his kingdom." And Madame, Louis xiv's sister-in-law, in 1701 recalled with obvious pleasure how time had offered her the most effective of vengeances: "[...] those who I once knew as beautiful are now more ugly than I; no living soul would recognise Mme de la Vallière; Mme de Montespan has skin like paper children play with, continually folding it and unfolding it again. Her entire face is covered with little wrinkles so close together that it is astonishing; her lovely hair is white as snow and her whole face is red [...]."

Opposite page:
Madame de la Vallière
(*Louise-Françoise
de la Baume-le-Blanc,
represented as in
the company of Diana*),
after Claude Lefebvre.

WHILE MADAME DE LA VALLIÈRE and Madame de Montespan were famous mistresses, others have remained forever unknown. The loves of the kings follow very special routes, behind the scene, and one of them leads to the Parc-aux-Cerfs (the Stags' Park). The name referred to an area of land but also, more importantly, to a house.

ONE DAY, Madame du Hausset, maid to the Marquise de Pompadour, was called to the king's cabinet room by her mistress who, with "a serious attitude", was walking up and down. Madame demanded that her maid go to the avenue de Saint-Cloud to help a young woman from the Parc-aux-Cerfs. This was a house on the corner of the rue de la Tournelle and the rue Saint-Méric, with four rooms downstairs and up, and where young and pretty women gathered. It is linked by a door to the Hôtel des Gardes (the Guards' House). It was therefore relatively simple to pretend a visit to the Guards' house and then to slip into the neighbouring house. Madame de Hausset was told the young woman was pregnant. "The father is a very honest man," said the king, to which the marquise added: "loved by everyone and adored by those who know him." It was not difficult for Madame de Hausset to guess who the father was. The bastard child of what the king called "a very good girl who was hardly a bright spark" would never be recognised, although would receive an allowance of some 10,000 or 12,000 livres. When Madame de Hausset dared ask Madame de Pompadour if the young expectant mother knew her child's father was the king, the latter replied: "I do not think so, but as he appeared to like this one, we are worried that others will be keen to tell her as much; that aside, we have told her and others that he is a Polish nobleman, a relative of the queen, and who has an apartment at the palace. That was imagined because of the blue sash that the King does not often have time to remove, because he would have to change clothes, and to give a reason for him having lodging at the palace, so close to the King."

Opposite page:
*The Marquise de
Montespan, mistress
of Louis XIV, after* Pierre
Mignard, circa 1694.

WHEN LOUIS XV was stabbed by Damien, the distress shown by the young woman from the Parc-aux-Cerfs, who Madame du Hausset mockingly

Above:
*Mademoiselle de
la Vallière and her
children,* Sir Peter Lely.

called 'Mother Abbess', revealed that she knew very well that the 'Polish prince' was the king. Some little while later, when the king returned to the house to climb to the room of one of her rivals, she threw herself at his feet. "Yes, you are the King of the entire kingdom, but that would be for nothing to me if you were not none of that in my heart. Do not abandon me, dear Sire."

But she perhaps ignored that at Versailles it is the fate of mistress to become abandoned. Madame de Pompadour's maid knew this fact better than anyone: "Apart from his little mistresses at the Parc-aux -Cerfs, the King sometimes had adventures with the women of Paris, or with women of the court who wrote to him." It required talent to stay close to the king when one had been dismissed as his mistress.

Left:
Madame de Montespan, the Duke of the Maine, the Count of Véxin, Mademoiselle de Nantes and Mademoiselle de Tours, after Pierre Mignard.

Madame de Maintenon

"She was no longer in the strength of youth; but she had such vivacious eyes, so brilliant, and her face shone with such a sparkling spirit when she spoke of action, that it was difficult to see her often without being drawn to her," wrote the Abbot of Choisy. "The King, used to the company of women since his earliest childhood, was delighted to have found one who spoke only of virtue; he had no fear whatsoever that it was said that she governed him. He found her modest and incapable of abusing the familiarity she enjoyed with the master." The subject of this gushing description by the abbot was Madame de Maintenon, written at the time she took control over Louis XIV. Madame de Caylus also approved the king's choice: "In her the King found a woman who was always modest, always mistress of her emotions, always herself, and who joined to these rare qualities the charms of the mind and conversation." These words of praise were not, however, the opinion of everyone.

She was held in contempt by Pierre Narbonne, Louis XIV's former valet, who became a police commissioner under the Régence, and who enjoyed spilling gossip about her in his *Journal*, which he established in 1701. Saint-Simon was another who disliked her, calling her "an old hag". Madame, the king's sister-in-law, hated her as much. In 1688 she wrote: "This woman is a nasty devil that everyone seeks and fears much, but she is little liked." In August, 1691, upon the death of Louvois, Madame wrote again: "For my part, I would have been happier that an old piece of filth would have died [...]." Year after year, Madame designates Madame de Maintenon by so many obstinately vicious names. In 1692, she calls her "an old *ripopée*", a term that refers to old wine so fermented that it borders on vinegar. In 1696 she wrote: "The old filth knows very well how to govern her man and remain his mistress." In 1701 and 1710 she is occasionally tamer, with mentions of "the reigning lady" and "the all-powerful lady", but the theme of "filth" peppers other correspondence.

Opposite page:
"Sincerity":
Ladies of the court
and abbot of the court,
in front of a mirror,
Henri Bonnart.

"I must admit that I am very angry with the king for treating me like a maid. It would suit his Maintenon; she is born for such a role, but not I…"*

Madame, Duchess of Orleans, née Princess Palatine

MADAME DE MAINTENON introduced boredom into court. On October 1st, 1687, Madame complained: "The court is becoming so boring, because the King believes himself devout if he ensures that we are bored." Some months later, on April 14th, 1688, it was more of the same. "The court is becoming so tiresome with all its continual hypocrisies that it is almost unbearable, and while people are irritated and exhausted to the bone, to carry them (as they put it) to virtue and the fear of God, the King chooses the most depraved beings in the world." The reign of boredom at court lasted 30 years, until the death of the king in 1715. Madame de Maintenon may have wanted to impose it for the sake of humility, as the following maxim of hers suggests: "Philosophy puts us above grandeur, but nothing places us above boredom."

TWO OTHER MAXIMS may explain the length of her own reign: "Abnegation resolves many problems of feminine existence" and "For women, gentleness is the best manner with which to get what one wants." Doubtless, she knew how to deprive herself as well as she knew how to be gentle with the king.

MADAME DE MAINTENON'S Maintenon's reign began in the greatest secrecy, during the night of October 9th, 1683. That was when Louis XIV, widow of Maria Theresa, who had passed away earlier that year on July 30th, married Madame de Maintenon, widow of Paul Scarron, who died in 1660. Since 1669 she had been in charge of ensuring the education of the children born from the relationship between Madame de Montespan and the king, and who were only recognised by him in 1673. For a long time, the marriage between the king and widow Scarron remained a secret, but eventually rumours spread. On May 13th, 1687, Madame wrote on the subject in reply top a question from the Duchess of Hanover: "You desire to know if it is true that the king has married Mme de Maintenon. I really cannot tell you if that is so. Few people doubt it. As for me, as long as the fact has not been announced, I will have difficulty believing it." She later had to resign herself to it and suffer in anger, because "this old girl is nasty, despite an outward appearance of devotion and humility."

Madame de Pompadour

THE DESCRIPTION OF HER BY DUFORT DE CHEVERNY EXPLAINS PERFECTLY WHY THE KING COULD NOT HAVE REMAINED INDIFFERENT TO HER CHARMS: "VERY WELL BUILT, SHE HAD A ROUND FACE, ALL HER FEATURES WERE REGULAR, A MAGNIFICENT COMPLEXION, THE HANDS AND ARMS WERE SUPERB, HER EYES WERE MORE PRETTY THAN WIDE, BUT SO SPARKLING, SO SPIRITUAL, WITH A BRILLIANCE I HAVE NEVER SEEN IN ANY OTHER WOMAN."* And the Cardinal de Bernis was of the same opinion: "Madame d'Etiolles had all the graces, all the freshness, and all the gayness of youth; she danced, sung and acted marvellously; she wanted for none of the pleasing talents; She enjoyed literature and arts; she had a high, sensitive and generous soul [...]."* It would therefore seem impossible for her to escape the attention of the king when, in February, 1745, she came to the court for the first time at the age of 23, for the occasion of the marriage between the dauphin Louis-Ferdinand and the Infant of Spain.

HER MAID, MADAME DE HAUSSET knew Madame de Pompadour better than any other woman at court, which allowed her this comment: "I am sorry for you, Madame, while everyone else is jealous of you." There was wisdom in Madame de Pompadour's answer: "Ah! My life is like that of a Christian, one of perpetual combat; this was not the case of those persons who succeeded in winning the good favour of Louis XIV; Madame de La Vallière allowed herself to be cheated upon by Madame de Montespan, but it was her own fault or, to put it better, the product of her kindness; she had no suspicions, at first, because she could not imagine her friend was perfidious. Madame de Montespan was shaken by Madame de Fontanges, and supplanted by Madame de Maintenon; but her haughtiness and her whims alienated the king. What is more, unlike me she had no rivals; but their lowness affords me safety, and in general I have only infidelities to fear of, and the difficulty of finding ways of rendering them occasional. The King likes change, but he is held also by habit; he fears outbursts, and detests intrigues; the marshal's wife said to me one day; it's your stairway that the king likes, he is used to climbing and descending it." That comment by the wife of the Marshal

Opposite page:
Portrait of
Madame de Pompadour,
François Boucher, 1750.

of Mirepoix was more evidence of the importance at Versailles of a world behind the scenes.

THE STAIRWAY in question was not Madame de Pompadour's only card. In fact, it ceased to be one when she was to move from the north top storey for another. Despite this move, she remained known for many as "la Poisson", for her real name was Jeanne Antoinette Le Normant d'Étioles, née Poisson ('Poisson' is also the French noun meaning 'fish'). She became the Marquise de Pompadour in only 1745. There was even a joke circulating at the time that went: "It was once before from Versailles / That came things of good taste / But today it is the rabble / Who reign and sit upon high / If the court is now so low / How could this astonish? / It is after all from the market / That comes to us our fish "*

WHILE THAT AND OTHERS like it were doing the rounds at court, Madame de Pompadour was the target of other attacks. In his *Journal*, the Marquis d'Argenson was pleased to record that some were "working on a wonderful genealogy of Mme de Pompadour and her brother Marigny. Their name is Poisson, and their coat-of-arms are fish; now, the sovereigns of Bar had for their coat-of-arms fish with a silver tiller, and a story has been composed to prove that our Poissons were a younger branch of the family who, at one time, fell out with their reigning elders and who were unjustly deprived of their tiller; titles have been made up and there you have the folly of those raised by fortune at court."*

THE SAME MARQUIS appeared to take pleasure in recounting the hatching of plots against her: "Ministers are cunningly creating rumours that the Marquise de Pompadour becomes their prime minister, and that they are going to work under her; it is a well meditated political plan by this inner circle, and thought up to turn the King off his favourite, with whom he no longer takes his pleasures."* But the plot failed. One year later, in 1756, the marquis observed: "The Marquise de Pompadour

Opposite page:
Madame de Pompadour,
Jean-Marc Nattier, 1748.

remains powerful in influence, although she no longer has the function of mistress, having become the centre of royal consolations concerning affairs." The Duke of Nivernais raged: "This woman who is not a minister is more than those who are because she has among her functions that of the department of favours. One must therefore avoid treating her lightly. Women who involve themselves with affairs like to be treated as seriously as the most serious men of State." Despite the power that is hers, Madame de Pompadour failed to bring into favour the French writer and philosopher Voltaire, even though he took the trouble of dedicating to her his tragedy *Tancrede*. Louis xv would have none of it and Madame de Pompadour did not insist.

HER POSITION at Versailles was only shaken by the stabbing of Louis xv by Damien, on January 5th, 1757, in the Marble Courtyard. A few hours after the attack, Cardinal de Bernis found "the court more preoccupied with what should be happening to Madame de Pompadour than the King's grievous accident. Will she leave? Will we see her again? Those were the things upon which the attention of the court appeared principally fixed." Soon rumours began circulating that she was connected to the attempt on the king's life. And if she was innocent of such accusations, the devout were content with suggesting that the loose ways to which she had led the monarch were the reason for his suffering divine punishment. Kept at a distance from the king, she informed his minister, the Duke of Choiseul: "He lives, I do not care about anything else. Cabals, indignities, the written notes, etc., nothing will scare me and I will serve him, whatever must happen to me, as long as I am in a position to do so." At last, the king wrote to her, the intrigues subsided and, observed Cardinal de Bernis "each one went about making up with the marquise, who, since that time, took a greater ascendancy and involved herself more than ever before in the affairs of State." He influence ended with her death on April 15th, 1764. It was raining that day in Versailles, and the king, sadly, commented: "The marquise will not have good weather for her journey."

"Happy were the times when reigned
  Louis and Pompadour!
Happy times when each one
  in France busied themselves
With nothing but verses, novels,
  music and dance,
The prestige of the arts
  and the sweet things of love!"*
Chamfort

Upstairs, downstairs

THESE STAIRS (PICTURED OPPOSITE) ALLOWED THE KING, FOLLOWING THE VERY OFFICIAL RITUAL OF RETIRING, TO REJOIN HIS MISTRESS IN HER BEDROOM. THEY WERE PART OF THE BEHIND-THE -SCENES WORLD OF VERSAILLES, AND MAY HAVE BEEN, UNDER LOUIS XV, THE STAGE FOR THE FOLLOWING INCIDENT RELATED BY MADAME DE POMPADOUR'S MAID, MADAME DU HAUSSET, IN HER MEMOIRS: "AN EVENT THAT MADE ME TREMBLE, JUST AS IT DID MADAME, EARNED ME FAMILIARITY WITH THE KING." Right in the middle of the night, Madame came into my room, which was alongside hers, in her nightgown and despairingly said to me: 'Come quickly, the King is dying.' One can imagine my fright. I took a petticoat, and I found the King in his bed, panting for breath. What could be done? It was indigestion. We threw water on him and he came to. I made him swallow some Hoffman's drops, and he said to me; "Let's not make any noise, just go to Quesnay, [François Quesnay was a doctor and economist] tell him it's your mistress who has been taken ill, and tell these people not to talk about it." Quesnay's lodgings were just nearby; he came immediately and was quite astonished to see the King thus. He took his pulse and said; 'The attack is over. But if the King had sixty years it could have been serious'. He went back to his quarters to search for some medicines and came back shortly afterwards and inundated the King with fragrances; I have forgotten the remedy that Dr. Quesnay made him take, but the effect was marvellous; I believe that it was some drops of general La Motte. I woke a wardrobe girl to make some tea for him and me; the King took three cups, put on his dressing gown, his stockings, and went to his apartment, helped by the doctor. What a performance, to see all three of us half-naked. Madame, as soon as possible, put on a dress, and the King changed himself, behind his curtains closed in all decency. He chatted about his short illness, and showed great thankfulness for the treatment we had administered to him. More than one hour later, I again felt the greatest terror, by thinking of how the king could die among us. Fortunately he came to himself so soon, and nobody knew, among the servants, what had happened to him."

Opposite page:
The staircase known
as 'the staircase
of mistresses'.
Following double-page:
The gate separating the
Courtyard
of Honour from the
Royal Courtyard
(also Louvre Courtyard).

The Enlightenment of Versailles

ENLIGHTENMENT CAME TO VERSAILLES, but not without difficulty. If Queen Maria Leszczynska attended a performance in Fontainebleau, in 1753, of the opera *Le Devin du Village (The Village Soothsayer)* she could not prevent herself from being "angry that it is Jean-Jacques Rousseau who created this work," adding: "It is quite true that he should never have done anything else but that!" Her husband, Louis XV, was well aware that the perceived grandeur of the reign of his father was in part due to the protection he gave to writers but he was nothing other than irritated by Voltaire. According to Madame du Hausset, he said: "For the rest, I treated him as well as Louis XIV treated Racine and Boileau; I gave him, as Louis XIV gave to Racine, the rank of an ordinary gentleman and pensions; it is not my fault if he does foolish things, and if he has the pretension of becoming a chamberlain, to have a cross and to sup with a King. It is not the fashion in France […]."

JEAN-FRANÇOIS MARMONTEL close to both Madame de Pompadour and to Cardinal de Bernis, regretted Louis XV's attitude towards Voltaire, whom he abandoned to an exile in Geneva. Marmontel writes in his *Memoirs*: "The response from the King 'Let him stay there' had not been properly thought beforehand. The exile he should have been given was to Versailles, where he would have been less daring than in Switzerland and Geneva. The priests should have opened up this magnificent prison to him […]." The light did not reach Versailles in the form of literature and ideas, no doubt because it would have been imprisoned there. What's more, numerous were those who thought like French dramatist and songwriter Charles Collé, whose plays and songs met with success. Concerning these philosophers and encyclopédistes (the Enlightenment group surrounding Denis Diderot and Jean le Rond d'Alembert who edited the *Encyclopédie*), Collé judged that they were "people of wide knowledge, that they have mind and method, sound judgement when passion is not involved, but have nothing of what is called genius; that in one word they have invented nothing, and that finally they have an insupportable ego […]." Versailles decided it could see quite well without them.

THE COUNT D'HÉZECQUES via the sciences. Louis XIV was most careful not to dismiss the great advances of this discipline under his reign. In 1744, he summoned Jean-Antoine Nollet, a French physicist and clergymen also known as abbot Nollet, a member of France's Royal Academy of Sciences, to give lessons in experimental physics to the dauphin. In 1758, when he was appointed physics and history master to the royal children, he was invited to set-up a laboratory in the Hôtel des Menus Plaisirs (the Entertainment and Ceremonies Office).

Above:
Louis XVI giving instructions to La Pérouse, Nicolas Monsiau, 1817.

UNDER THE REIGN OF LOUIS XIV, wrote of the existence, in the Salon of Apollo, of a throne sitting under a crimson canopy of damask and which had never been used for any audience. "In this same room was, attached to the window, a crystal thermometer which the King, several times a day, would check the temperature with." How, indeed, would it have been possible not to be fascinated by this instrument that Monsieur de Réaumur had produced and which Monsieur Celsius had perfected with the use of mercury in 1742? How could the king not have received Monsieur Étienne de Montgolfier who proposed flying, before his eyes, a balloon filled with hot air and which would carry animals in a gondola? And so it was that, on September 19th, 1783, the invention took to the skies above Versailles, flying for some ten minutes at a height of around 500 metres and carrying with it a duck, a cock and a sheep. It was perhaps the very first time a king had seen a sheep, if not a pig, fly! Jean-François de Galaup, Count of La Pérouse, was introduced to Louis XVI by his navy minister, the Marquis de Castries, which led the king to grant him several boats with which to accomplish his project of sailing around the world.

LOUIS XVI admired craftsmanship, and spent part of his leisure time making metal pieces, including locks, in a workshop in the palace helped and advised by Versailles locksmith François Gamain. The admiration and flattery that the locksmith directed towards the king should have put him on guard. Perhaps the monarch paid too little attention to the craftsman's declaration to the king one day in the workshop: "Sire, when Kings involve themselves with the works of the people, the people involve themselves in the works of king!" Louis XVI would be reminded of these words during his trial. For it was Gamain who, after the revolution in 1792, revealed to Interior Minister Jean-Marie Roland the existence of a secret safe, built and installed by the king behind the walls of a corridor in the Tuileries, between his room and that of the dauphin. It was Gamain who the king had commissioned to fit an iron door to protect the safe,

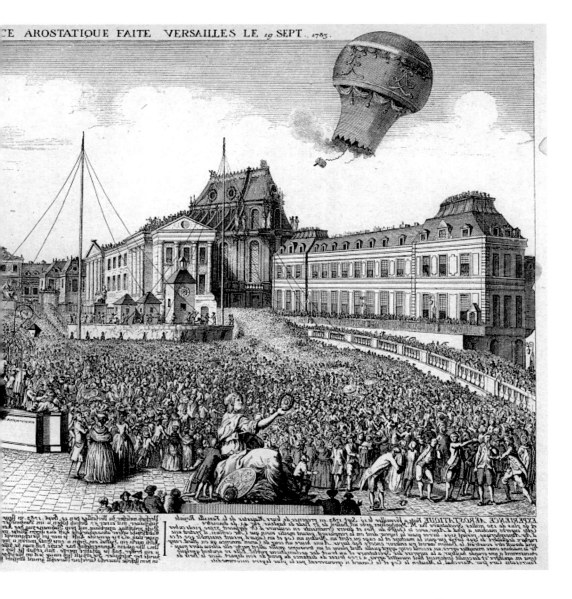

complete with hinges and plates. The documents found inside were used as damming evidence at his trial, which ended with his head falling into a basket on January 21st, 1793.

Above:
An aerostatic
experiment held
at Versailles,
September 19th, 1783.

The faces of Glory

Several bookcases in Versailles contain a copy of *Iconology or the New Explanation of Several Images, Emblems and Other Figures...* — the title continues for another ten lines — *From Research and Figures by César Ripa, Moralized by J. Baudoin.* Since its publication in 1644 by Mathieu Guillemot, (situated 'rue Saint Jacques, on the corner of the rue de la Parcheminerie'), this book has become indispensable reading for the understanding of allegories about "virtues, vices, arts, sciences, natural causes, different moods and human passions." In this dictionary, of which the first part covers *'Abundancy to Zeal'*, figures the 'Glory of Princes', which was not to be confused with 'Glory': "The invention of this figure is taken from one of the most wonderful medals of the emperor Hadrian. It has on the head a rich gold crown, and holds another in laurel leaves with the right hand, while the left hand holds a pyramidal object. The gold crown represents the reward that great princes receive for the worthy enterprises that they are forever busy with, and the great actions that follow these. That of laurel is an illustrious prize, which they themselves give as a mark of honour to those who follow them, in recognition of their valour. The pyramid is also a symbol of their glory, which shines in various forms from their temples and rich palaces that they build with royal magnificence. For these superb indications of their grandeur render them recognisable for posterity, over a long number of years. Which is what is also illustrated in the prodigious masses of stone that remain of the pyramids in Egypt and which time, however injurious it may be, has not been able to demolish, nor prevent from being, as in the past, among the world's miracles, to the glory of their makers."*

The sculpture (pictured left) of Glory, probably the work of Thomas Regnaudin in 1678 or 1679, stands on the corners of the Marble Courtyard and the Royal Courtyard. The artist perfectly followed the description by Baudoin, except for one detail. A restoration carried out on it at the beginning of the 19th Century revealed that the crown on the head of this Glory is not in gold but made up of lilies, like those on the king's blazon. This 'Glory of Princes' is that of the French king.

Opposite page:
The King gives orders for a simultaneous attack on four Dutch fortified towns, 1672, on the ceiling of the Hall of Mirrors, Charles Le Brun, 1680 to 1684.

It was thus not by chance that in 1734, Jean-François de Troy painted the dauphin, when he was aged five years, surrounded by his sisters in front of a pyramid. Similarly, a pyramid appears again in the 1782 painting *The royal family altogether around the dauphin Louis-Joseph-Xavier-François*, and its presence alone is all that is needed to signify glory. But what would be the glory for he who will never be Louis XVII? The child, sitting on the knees of his mother Marie-Antoinette and upon whom his father Louis XVI gently rests his hand, will never be Louis XVII because his uncle, the Count of Provence, who is leaning from behind the sofa upon which the king is sitting, had taken the name Louis XVIII.

Below:
Members of the royal family of France together with the dauphin born in 1781.

Above:
*The children of France
swept by Glory,*
Jean-François de Troy,
1735.

"You love only your glory
and your comfort."*
Fénelon addressing Louis XIV

The Estates-General

ON AUGUST 8TH, **1788,** THE KING RESIGNED HIMSELF TO CONVENING THE ESTATES **-GENERAL,** a general assembly that represented three 'Orders', or sections of French society. There had not been such a meeting since 1614. Representatives of the three orders – the clergy (First Estate), the nobility (Second Estate) and (theoretically) the rest of the population (Third Estate) – were notified on January 14th, 1789, that the king invited his loyal subjects to help him "overcome all the difficulties in which we find Ourselves relative to the state of Our finances, and to establish, according to Our wishes, a constant and invariable order in all the parties of government which are interested by the happiness of Our subjects and the prosperity of Our kingdom."* On May 5th, 1789, following a procession and a mass, the opening session began in what was the Hall of Entertainment and Ceremonies (salle des Menus Plaisirs), re-named the Hall of the Three Orders. With the clergy seated at his right, and the nobility seated at his left, the king, facing the Third Estate, began his address: "The hope that I had of seeing all the Orders united in sentiment to work with me for the general good of the State has not been abused." Why would he doubt that his people loved him? Only pessimists would pay any attention to the injurious quatrains circulating at the time, like this one that appeared to target Marie-Antoinette: The time will come when France, imprudent belle / After suffering so much that could have been averted / Will recreate before you the horror of Dante's Hell / Queen, that day is nigh, and you have been here alerted. *

So IT WAS that the king serenely addressed the Estates with this wish: "Gentlemen, let that this assembly reaches happy agreement, and this epoch should become for ever memorable for the happiness and prosperity of the kingdom. I will it from my heart, it is the most ardent of my wishes, it is at last the prize that I wait upon for the honesty of my intentions, and for my love for my people." There followed a speech by the Justice Minister Charles de Paule de Barentin, and then, during another by Finance Minister Jacques Necker, which lasted more than two hours in which he detailed the disastrous state of finances, the king fell asleep.

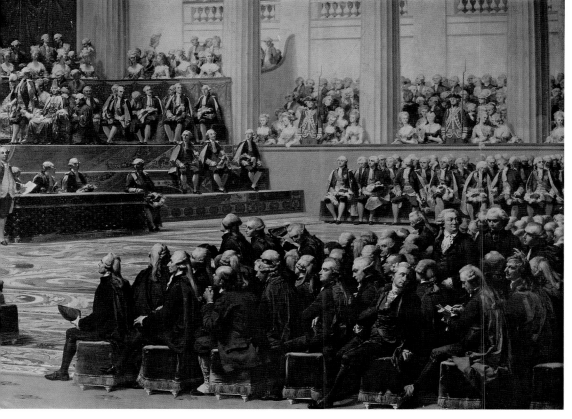

THAT EVENING, Louis xv's daughter Madame Adélaïde enquired of the Marquis d'Osmond why he had not taken part in the Assembly meeting. "It is that I dislike funerals, Madame," he answered bluntly, "and that of the monarchy in particular."

Above:
Meeting of the Estates-General at Versailles, May 5th, 1789, Auguste Couder, 1839.

BETWEEN APRIL AND DECEMBER 1875, in the central court of the south-facing wing of the palace, the architect Edmond de Joly built for the Third Republic a hall large enough for members of parliament to meet with senators to elect a president of the republic. Above the speakers' platform, a vast canvas painting was placed in such a manner that none of those gathered in the hall could avoid seeing it. It depicts the opening session of the Estates-General on May 5th, 1789. Painted in 1891 by Ferdinand Bassot, it was a copy of an original painting commissioned in 1840 by Louis-Philippe from Auguste Couder (1790-1873). It is thus before an image of what did indeed turn out to be the funeral rites of the monarchy that the French Republic elected 14 of its presidents; these included 12 presidents under the Third Republic and the two presidents of the Fourth republic. Meanwhile, the current Fifth Republic continues to meet before the painting for Congress meetings uniting members of parliament and senators.

Right:
A harp that belonged
to Marie-Antoinette.
Opposite page:
Marie-Antoinette,
surrounded by her
court, playing the pedal
harp for her friends
in her music room in
Versailles, 1777.

The Revolution

"THE WHOLE OF FRANCE IS NO LONGER ANYTHING OTHER THAN A GREAT SORRY HOSPITAL WITHOUT ANY PROVISIONS." That alarming observation by Fénelon in a letter he wrote to Louis XIV in 1694 was still as pertinent some one hundred years later. After the opening of the Estates-General on May 5th, 1789, events took a rapid course, beginning with the refusal of representatives of the Third Estate to meet other than in the presence of the clergy and the nobility. Soon after, the clergy's parish priests had joined them. On June 20th, after they were unable to meet in the Hall of Entertainment and Ceremonies, closed by order of the king, the representatives met in the Hall of Tennis (salle du Jeu de Paume). It was there that they vowed together "never to separate ourselves, to meet wherever circumstances demanded, and this until a time when the Constitution of the kingdom be established and reinforced upon solid grounds."*

THE NEXT DAY, the Count of Vaudreuil warned the queen: "Madame, it is not the beginning of a revolt, it is a revolution underway; I see it as done this morning!" to which the queen replied: "And you dare tell me that to my face!" – "Oh, Madame, is it a crime to have you hear the truth?" – "No, sir, on the contrary, I thank you for it [...] You see how one falls from upon high when one wakes up queen and goes to bed...what? What will I be tonight?" The count was careful not to reply. She could certainly not have imagined that on the morning of October 16th, 1793, she would be taken from the Conciergerie, her arms tied behind her back, to a public place where a guillotine had been erected, the same that had decapitated Louis XVI that same year, on January 21st.

ON JUNE 23rd, 1789, the Third Estate was involved in a further affront towards the king who, at the end of a speech in which he had proposed a number of reforms, concluded: "I give you order, Gentlemen, to separate immediately and for each of you to go tomorrow morning to the chamber of your Order and recommence your sessions." The Third Estate could only see in this that the king wanted to finish with the Estates-General,

Above:
*The Gentlemen of the Third Estate at the session of
June 23rd, 1789,* Lucien Melingue, 1874.

that which he himself had convened, and which now had ambitions to become a National Assembly, on the lines of a parliament. While the nobles obeyed the monarch, the Third Estate refused to leave the hall. The Marquis de Dreux-Brézé was called upon to reiterate the king's order. He was told that "the Nation assembled cannot be given orders" and the Marquis de Mirabeau, representative of the Third Estate, gave his own orders: "Slave, go and tell your master the we, representatives of France, are here by the will of the people and this will only be taken from us by the power of bayonets!" When the king was informed of this, he sighed: "Oh, what the devil! Let them stay!"

A rumour quickly spread that the king had assembled his troops to break-up and arrest the representatives, who now had aspirations to form a veritable parliament. But in fact, his sentiment was of a different tack; "I do not want blood to flow," he is reported to have said," I love my people; they are sure of my love; everything will sort be alright; those who live of abuse shout and claim that all is lost; that will not be the case." But he was wrong. On July 14th the Bastille was stormed by the people of Paris who put an end to that odious symbol of arbitrary arrest warrants. On the night of July 16th, some began to flee Versailles. The Countess of Adhémar observed: "During that first moment the court was worse than a desert; people left by night under borrowed names."

"The abuses, which began with the arrogant pride of Louis XIX, lead necessarily to the downfall of the kingdom."* Marquis d'Argenson

Above:
Salle du Jeu de Paume (Hall of Tennis). In the foreground is a sculpture of Jean-Sylvain Bailly, president of the session of June 17th, in the centre is a sculpture of the Bastille, carved from a stone from the Bastille itself, while in the background is a copy of the painting by Jacques-Louis David of the *Oath of the Jeu de Paume*.

Above:
Preparatory drawings for the *Oath of the Jeu de Paume*, Jacques-Louis David.

BARELY ONE MONTH LATER, everything appeared to have irrevocably collapsed. During the night of August 4th, the three estates voted for the abolition of all privileges, including those accorded to nobles and the clergy just as those granted to towns and provinces. Soon after, the queen exclaimed: "I am astonished that Messers de Noailles, d'Aiguillon and de Montmorency have not yet asked for the throne to be overturned; they would have been accorded this with acclamation; in any case, it is ready to fall, it has no support." The king wrote to the Archbishop of Arles: "If I was forced to take sanction, then I would give way, but if that happened France would no longer have a monarchy or monarch."

FORCE ENTERED THE STAGE when the people of Paris travelled to Versailles on October 5th, and the next day the king had no other choice than to return to the capital. Was there still a monarchy, or a monarch in France? Whatever, from that day on there would no longer be either at Versailles.

FINDING HIMSELF BACK at Versailles during the regime of the Consulate (1799 – 1804), the Count d'Hézecques beheld at the abandoned palace where once he had been a page: "Everything is crumbling," he lamented. "The ripped gates are a reminder of the crimes; those visible remains of magnificence are a painful reminder of the splendour of the place. One looks for the masters of these vast domains, and then one shudders to think that they disappeared with the speed of lightening."

Winning the battle
by compromise

Below:
Louis-Philippe is presented with the members of the diplomatic corps in the Hall of Battles, during the inauguration of the Versailles museum, June 10th, 1837 François-Joseph Heim.

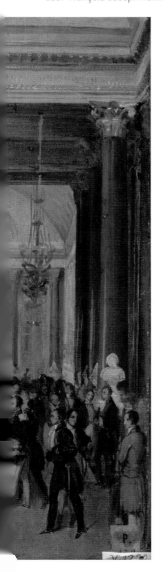

HE WAS HATED BY THE LEGITIMISTS BECAUSE HE WAS THE SON OF PHILIPPE ÉGALITÉ, THE DUKE OF ORLEANS, WHO VOTED FOR THE EXECUTION OF THE KING. THEY HATED HIM ALSO BECAUSE HE SIDED WITH THOSE WHO DEPOSED LOUIS XVI ON AUGUST 10TH, 1792, BY FIGHTING FOR THE REPUBLICAN ARMY AGAINST THE PRUSSIANS AT THE BATTLE OF VALMY ON SEPTEMBER 20TH, 1792, AND AGAIN AGAINST THE AUSTRIANS ON NOVEMBER 6TH THAT SAME YEAR AT JEMMAPES. HE WAS LOUIS-PHILIPPE, BORN ON OCTOBER 6TH, 1773, AND HE BECAME KING OF FRANCE FOLLOWING THE 1830 JULY REVOLUTION. As he mounted the throne, his hope was that the revolution had put a definitive end to the power of the Bourbons, those who had only allowed him to return to France in 1817. He arrived from Britain, where he had chosen to exile himself instead of in Belgium, at Ghent, to where Louis XVIII had previously fled. The Countess d'Adhémar had no doubt that if he had adopted the blue, white and red colours of the republican and Bonapartist armies, it was because they were, above all, those of the Orleans. "They tell simpletons that it was bits from the blazon of the coat of arms of the town [Paris], with the silver prows and rig of antique boats, with the blue top stitched with countless lilies, but in reality, those who knew said they were carrying the colours of the servants of the house of Orleans; they had red garments, white jackets and blue knee-breeches, if my memory is correct, and their braid was at least white and blue."

TO COME FROM the family of Orleans, a descendent of Louis XVI's youngest brother, Philip of France, who was born in 1640, meant one would meet with opposition from the republicans, Bonapartists and naturally the Legitimists, who were outraged at the move to put Louis-Philippe on the throne after Charles X had abdicated in favour of his grandson Henri, Duke of Bordeaux. It was a hugely symbolic gesture by Louis-Philippe to dedicate the palace of Versailles, as a museum, "to all the glories of France" and, going beyond what such Glories (with a capital 'G') owed to the monarchy, to introduce there the heroic figures of the Republic and the Empire; just as it was for him to return the title (first used following the Reign of Terror) of 'Place de la Concorde' to the main Paris square that once carried the names of Louis xv, the Revolution, and Louis xvi. The transformation of Versailles into a national museum brought with it the sacrifice of the apartments of the princes and courtesans in the south-facing wing of the palace, part of numerous changes carried out over some 10 years by the architects Pierre-François-Léonard Fontaine and Eugène-Charles-Frédérique Nepveu.

WHEN THE HALL OF BATTLES (galerie des Batailles) was inaugurated in1837, celebrating the major French military battles from that of Tolbiac (in 496) to that of Wagram (in 1809), there was great ceremony; no flags or halberds were missing, and the troops and their horses were as impeccable as could be. The Countess of Boigne said of the event "it was the palace of Louis xiv overrun by the bourgeoisie", but most opin-ion approved the king's project – as did even the countess, who wrote in her *Memoirs*: "Honour to the King who knew how to resuscitate it [Versailles] in as much as the circumstances allowed. There is only the nation in its entirety, today sufficiently grown into a grand lady, which can replace Louis xiv in his palace." Her view was shared by a 35 year-old poet named Victor Hugo (later made a Peer of France by Louis-Philippe in April, 1845), who wrote: "What King Louis-Philippe has done at Versailles is good. To have accomplished this work is to have been grand as a king and as impartial as a philosopher; it is to have given to this marvellous book that is the history of France this magnificent bind-ing that is called Versailles."* If the Hall of Battles was a political combat for Louis-Philippe, there was no doubt he had won it. Compromise was a small price to pay for his reign.

IT APPEARED TO TROUBLE FEW if any, present at Versailles that France's history had been reduced to its military victories, considered to be its only source of glory. Even fewer still are likely to have meditated the *Memoirs* of one Valentin Jamerey-Duval, who served for many years in the entourage of Francis III of Lorraine, who became Francis II of Tuscany before finally becoming Francis I, Holy Roman Emperor, in 1745. The emperor appointed Jamerey-Duval head of Imperial medals and coins, based in Vienna, Austria. Jamerey-Duval wrote of his French compatriots: "[…] despite the superiority that they lend themselves over every nation in terms of taste and flair, I do not see them having yet paid tribute to true merit in as solemn a manner as that which the Dutch have done in a square in Rotterdam, where they erected a bronze statue to honour the memory of their compatriot, Erasmus."

BUT FOR JUST SUCH GLORIES that owe nothing to war, the sculptor David d'Angers was, in 1837, finishing his work 'La Patrie' (The Homeland). It was to adorn the pediment of the Pantheon, once the church of Sainte-Geneviève and which was transformed into a place of tribute "to the great men of the homeland to whom we are grateful." During the reign of Louis XIV, Fénelon wrote: "To take away a field from an individual is a proper sin; to take a great country from a nation is innocent and glorious! Where have ideas of justice gone?" Pressing further, Fénelon demanded of the king: "Did you not think war was necessary so that you could take possession of places that suited you and which would ensure the safety of your frontiers? What a strange law! By these ways, from one place to the next, one will reach China!"

Revolutionary crusade

LOUIS-PHILIPPE CHOSE A CELEBRATED ARTIST WHEN IN **1838** HE COMMISSIONED A PAINTING TO DEPICT THE PROCESSION OF CRUSADERS BEFORE THE TAKING OF JERUSALEM IN **1099.** Jean -Victor Schnetz, born in Versailles in 1787, had become in 1837 a member of the Institute of France, and a member of the Académie des Beaux-Arts (Academy of Fine Arts). A student under David, and a friend of artist Théodore Géricault, he emerged unscathed from the battle between the classical and romantic schools. He managed this by painting romantic subjects in a classical style, and vice versa. In 1841, the year that he succeeded Jean Auguste Dominique Ingres at the Academy of France in Rome, which Louis XIV had created, he presented his painting to the Salon de Paris. It was greeted with great admiration, and was soon a part of the King of France's museum of Versailles, with the title: *Procession of Crusaders around Jerusalem, led by Pierre l'Ermite and Godefroy de Bouillon, the day before the attack on the town, July 14th, 1099.*

IN FACT, THOSE WHO LEFT for the Holy Land by the will of Pope Urban II, who at the council of Clermont in 1095 called for the tomb of Christ to be freed, those who undertook an 'iter hierosolymitanum', a journey to Jerusalem, a 'peregrinatio', or piligrimage, were not called crusaders until around 1250. The painting avoided any representation of those haggard men who arrived before the town on July 7th, exhausted by heat, thirst and hunger, with insufficient weapons and who were told that a hostile Fatimid army was on its way from Egypt. These were not expected of the painting, which was to represent glory. The anonymous author of *Gesta Francorum*, the Latin chronicle of the First Crusade, recorded: "On the Wednesday and the Thursday, we attacked the town from every side with force, but before we launched the assault, the bishops and priests had it decided by their sermons and exhortations that we would, in honour of God, proceed in a procession around the ramparts of Jerusalem, accompanied by prayers, almsgiving and fasting."* It is this moment, when the procession, having climbed the Mount of Olives, listens to the sermons of Pierre l'Ermite,

Above:
*Procession of Crusaders around Jerusalem, led by Pierre l'Ermite and Godefroy de Bouillon,
the day before the attack on the town, July 14th, 1099*, Jean-Victor Schnetz, 1841.

Raymond d'Aguilers and Arnulf de Malecorne, the chaplain of Robert of Normandy, that Schnetz captures in his painting.

HISTORICAL RECORDS SHOW THE PROCESSION was held on July 8th, and not on the 14th of the month, the day before the town was taken. But of course, since 1789, this date has major significance; July 14th, the day the Bastille was stormed, is the date of the Revolution of which the three united colours of blue, white and red have become the symbol. The French writer, the Count of Mirabeau, called them 'the livery of liberty". Following the 1830 revolution that chased Charles x from the throne, Louis-Philippe gave a speech at the Paris Town Hall in which he declared: "Returning to the town of Paris, I wore with pride the glorious colours that you have recovered, and that I have myself worn for a long time." It was therefore most certainly not by chance that Schnetz's painting of the crusaders shows that their banners, floating in the sky of the holy land that July 14th, 1099, were blue, white and red. The king-citizen could only have appreciated the homage.

Above:
The Hall of Crusades.
Opposite page:
Louis-Philippe, the royal family and king Leopold 1ˢᵗ visiting the Hall of Crusades of the palace of Versailles, in July 1844, Prosper Lafaye.

Above:
Entrance hall built in 1679 and situated on the ground floor of the palace, between the Marble Courtyard and the gardens.

Stage Right,
the Gardens

Alleyways, fountains and bosquets

IT IS HARDLY NOVEL TO SUGGEST THAT VERSAILLES WAS A WORLD OF THEATRE WHERE THE WINGS WERE, SEPARATELY, THE PALACE AND THE GARDENS. Indeed, the Duke of Saint-Simon was among the first to recognise this. He wrote: "From the court side, the strangeness was suffocating, and these vast wings ran along without any particular sense. On the garden side, one enjoyed the beauty of the entire ensemble, but it was like looking at a palace that had been burnt, where the last floor and the roofs were still missing." Nothing finds favour in the eyes of the duke: "There will never be an end to the monstrous defects of a palace so immensely expensive, with its accompaniments that are even more so: the orangery, vegetable gardens, kennels, the Great and Small Stables the same, what prodigious dependencies."*

WHILE LOUIS XIV LEFT IT TO OTHERS, like André Félibien ou Madame de Scudéry, to pen marvelous descriptions of the palace was, he took it upon himself to write *The Way to Present the Gardens of Versailles*. He was the guide during a visit in July 1689 of Mary of Modena, queen consort of James II and who sought exile in France after the English Revolution of 1688. In 1705 he prepared a sixth edition of the work. This was most likely done by dictation – unlike the fourth edition, which he wrote by his own hand and the fifth, which he corrected in similar manner – and left nothing for chance. It begins with the following words: "Leaving the palace by the hall of the Marble Courtyard, we take to the terrace; there must be a halt at the top of the steps to consider the view of the planted beds surrounding the water basins and the fountains of the Cabinets." The words "there must" indicate that the invitation is an order. The visit ends some 25 stages later. Having returned "to the palace by the marble step, one will turn at the top of the steps to look at the North parterres, the statues, the vases, the crowns, the pyramid and what can be seen of Neptune, and afterwards one leaves the gardens by the same door through which they were entered." The king does not exclude a visit the same day to the menagerie at the Trianon. Four years after the death of Louis XIV, in 1719, Hérisset and Sornique engraved a plan that precisely followed "the walk that the King had set out to

Above:
The gardens of Versailles as seen from one of the
windows of Mesdames, the daughters of Louis XV.

Right:
*View of the labyrinth
with Diana and her
nymphs,* Jean Cotelle,
after 1688.
Opposite page:
*View of the Arch
of Triumph and of France
triumphant with
nymphs enchaining
captives before Mars
and Venus,*
Jean Cotelle, 1688.

**Following page,
clockwise from top:**
*View of the bosket and
water theatre, or stage,
with nymphs preparing
to receive Psyche,*
Jean Cotelle, 1688.
*View of the Dragon
Pool and the ramp of
the Neptune Pool with
Apollo killing the serpent
Python,* Jean Cotelle.
*View of the colonnade
with Apollo and
the nymphs,*
Jean Cotelle, circa 1688.
*View of the Orangery,
seen from the Swiss
Pool and the King's
Vegetable Garden in
Versailles, in 1688-1691,*
Jean Cotelle.

present the garden, the boskets and the fountains of the aforesaid royal garden of Versailles." The walk was indeed a strictly planned affair, for the fountains gushed to match each stage of the visit.

In 1756, one visitor observed: "The water springing from the boskets of Versailles involve such a considerable volume of water when they are all performing together, that it is ordinarily the case in the summer, during the stay of the King in Versailles, to have only the water beds and ponds that can be see from the palace and the terraces working from ten o'clock in the morning until eight o'clock in the evening." Economising the water supply was necessary ever since the royal site was built. The orders given under Louis XIV leave no doubt about this: "When His Majesty arrives along the banks of the lake, there must be water supplied to the Pyramid Fountain, the Water Walk, and to the Dragon Pool, and precautions will be taken to ensure that the fountains perform to perfection for as long as they are within site of the King." But, as soon as "His Majesty has passed and is out of sight" all the valves and pumps were to be closed.

It was once again Louis XIV himself who dictated to Claude Perrault, on August 18th, 1672, his "order to be observed concerning the fountains of Versailles." The gardens were still far from completed. In 1677, the English philosopher John Locke, who had the privilege of accompanying the king during one of his walks in the gardens, joined also by Madame de Montespan, recorded: The king appeared very pleased with his fountains, and had made several changes which he indicated with his cane."* The fountain operators had scrupulously obeyed the changes demanded. The very strict regulations that governed them from 1672 demanded that they lodge in the Pump Room, at the king's disposition, and that they never leave it without the express permission of the superintendent. For if the king, at a whim, suddenly decided to go for a walk, they had to be ready at that same instant to open the valves and close them just as soon when the visit was over. Charles Perrault wrote in his *Memoirs* that "all that could contribute to providing water to Versailles was so sacred, and so welcome to the King, that Monsieur Colbert listened to everything with an inconceivable benignity and went to great trouble to verify everything that was proposed."

Above left:
View of the Arch of Triumph, with Venus welcoming Mars, Jean Cotelle, 1688.
Above right:
A perspective of the Three-Fountains, Jean Cotelle, 1688.

The Grotto of Thetis

CHARLES PERRAULT HAD A SUGGESTION: BECAUSE "MOST OF THE ORNAMENTS OF VERSAILLES CONCERNED THE FABLES OF THE SUN AND APOLLO", AND BECAUSE THERE HAD BEEN PLACED "A RISING SUN IN THE BASIN AT THE EXTREME END OF THE SMALL PARK" HE THOUGHT IT WOULD BE A GOOD IDEA "THAT AT THE OTHER EXTREMITY OF THIS SAME PARK WHERE THE GROTTO WAS (FOR IT HAS SINCE BEEN DEMOLISHED) IT WOULD BE GOOD TO PLACE AN APOLLO WHO, HAVING TRAVELLED AROUND THE WORLD, IS ABOUT TO REST IN THE PLACE OF THETIS, SO AS TO REPRESENT THE KING WHO HAS COME TO REST AT VERSAILLES AFTER HIS WORK IN GIVING GOOD TO EVERYONE." The first design for this project received royal approval and a second design by Le Brun served as a model to the sculptors Girardon and Regnaudin who formed an "Apollo in the large middle recess, where the nymphs of Thetis wash and bathe him." Based on the same design, Gaspard Marsi and Gilles Guérin sculpted groups of four horses, rubbed down by Tritons, which were placed in the adjoining recess. The brother of Charles Perrault designed "a sun of Gold that spread its beams, also gold, across the breadth of the three doors." Perrault concluded his account with a description of the grotto knocked down in 1684 to allow the building of the palace's North wing: "It seems that the sun was present in this grotto and that it was visible through the grill of the door."

IT WAS THANKS TO THREE RESERVOIRS, completed in 1667, that this same grotto had caused wonderment with its water display during a party given the following year for ambassadors and members of the court. Their joy was akin to the lines written by La Fontaine in *The Loves of Cupid and Psyche:* "The more these jets were a confused display, the more their beauty / Water crossed, joined, separated and came to unity / Recesses, hollows, there was no refuge / My muse is impotent to paint this deluge."* La Fontaine, who knows better than anyone that there is never a fable without a moral, added: "When the sun is there, and he has done his best / He descends to Thetis, and finds some rest / That is when Louis goes there to be refreshingly treated / With a joy that everyday must be repeated."*

Below:
*Louis XIV followed by the grand dauphin passing on
horseback before the Grotto of Thesis*, circa 1684.

THE GARDENS THAT LE NÔTRE, along with his architects, the first painter and the sculptors, organised, planned and decorated were dedicated to the glory of Louis the Great. As André Félibien wrote in his *Description of Versailles*: "It is important to note first that, because the sun is the King's watchword, and because poets confuse Apollo with the sun, there is nothing in this superb house that does not have a link with this divinity; it is thus that all the figures and ornaments that can be seen there, which are not positioned by chance, have a relationship with either the sun or the particular spots where they are placed."

THE SCULPTURES THAT WERE TAKEN FROM THE GROTTO when it was eventually destroyed found a place in another grotto, a work conceived in 1778 by the painter Hubert Robert, for the bosquet of Apollo. But it was as if it was no longer possible to be astonished by such works. Jean-François Marmontel, a close acquaintance of Madame de Pompadour, wrote in his *Memoirs*: "Would anyone believe it? These magnificent gardens were impracticable during the warm season. Especially when the heat came, these water courses, this lovely canal, these basins of marble, surrounded by statues that seemed to breathe bronze, exhaled for far afield the most putrid vapours; and the waters of Marly only came to this valley, at great cost, to stagnate and poison the air that we breathed."*

WHAT LA FONTAINE CALLED "the air that mortals did not have", had become unbreathable.

Below:
*The project plan for the bosket of the Grotto of Apollo
in the gardens of Versailles*, Hubert Robert, 1775.

Left:
*View of the Palace
of Versailles from
a water parterre,*
Perelle, 1670.

Leto, a lesson for all

"LETO AND HER TWINS/ AGAINST HARD, VULGAR PEOPLE OF VILE ANIMAL SINS / CHANGED THEM WITH WATER WHICH ONTO THEM THEY THREW / [...] THE SCENE IS A BASIN OF GREAT EXPANSE / THIS MOB WERE INTO INSECTS CHANGED ON THE BANKS / TRIED TO THROW WATER AGAINST DEITIES."* These verses of La Fontaine are based upon the account by the Roman poet Ovid, in book VI of his *Metamorphosis*, in which he recounts that "one day when the sky sent upon the countryside its devouring fire" Leto leans to drink from a source of pure water. But she is prevented by a "vulgar band" who are there cutting a field of reeds. Even her plea – "oh! Let you be softened by these two children who, attached to my breast, stretch their feeble arms towards you" – does not change the mob's behaviour. Soon, they escalate their injurious attitude towards the goddess, threatening "with their hands, their feet", they disturb the waters of lake, bringing all the filth of the bed to the surface. That was when the anger of the goddess - "Then live forever in the mire of the swamp!" – provoked their metamorphosis. Ovid's story ends with the description of these "vulgar shepherds" who "dive into the water. As soon, they disappear to the bottom of the pond; just as soon they swim at the surface. Quite often they jumped onto the banks; often they jumped into the water. And, shameless of their punishment, they went about outrageously exercising their vile language; even, under the water, one could hear their cries of insult towards Leto. But already their voices had become hoarse, their throats swollen, the mouths widening with their insults, their necks disappearing. Their heads joined their shoulders. Their backs became green, their bellies, which now formed the largest part of their bodies, whitened. Then, changed into frogs, they sprang towards the mud of the swamp."* This formidable Leto, who caused the metamorphosis into frogs of this rough group of shepherds from Lycia, is the mother of Apollo and Diana.

WHILE THE COURT SETTLED IN VERSAILLES, it was a clear lesson to be remembered for whoever passed beside the Basin of Leto. Whoever would affront her was also offending Apollo, her son. This was inadmissible and would not be

tolerated. To defy Leto was to challenge Apollo, who killed the python that persecuted her. He also, according to Homer's *Iliad*, exterminated the children of Niobe with his silver bow, after they had the impudence to pretend they were as beautiful as she. It was a strong message; the revolt of parliament and princes included the inadmissible audacity to threaten Anne of Austria, mother of Louis xiv. It was not difficult to liken the king – who at the age of 22 years had risen to power following the death of Cardinal de Mazarin – to Leto, who proned upon high over her water basin. But at Versailles, while no-one would be turned into a frog, they could fear a no less terrible fate: to be disgraced by the king.

THE WATER BASIN THAT THE COURTESANS gazed upon featured sculptures by the Marsi brothers, which only took on all their splendour when the powerful waters gushed forth, rushing from what was a tree-like structure of tubes. In 1672, a writer for the *Mercure Galant* enthused: "I would never be able to finish if I was to tell you of the marvels that the waters create in this delicious place. M. de Francine makes them do things that surpass imagination." The

Above:
The lead water pipes underneath the Basin of Leto.

Monsieur de Francine in question is probably the elder brother, François, who remained in the shade compared to the great landscape architect André Le Nôtre, the grand master of the gardens. Perhaps this was because de Francine's work was only visible below ground level, and inherently obscure.

PRIMI VISCONTI, *writing in his Memoirs on the court of Louis XIV*, mentions them both: "Concerning the garden with its fountains, this is a marvellous thing. A certain Le Nôtre is the designer, and what is all the more amazing is that he did this without schooling, and from his own remarkable talent, for he was before this a simple gardener. The hydraulic engineer is a certain Francini, [Francine] son of a Florentine, of large corpulence, but of even larger mind. He costs the King much, because he is quite ignorant concerning the execution of Le Nôtre's plans. Just for the aqueducts, he is blamed with burying lead worth more than seven million."

Untamed nature

ARRIVING IN VERSAILLES AS ONE OF THE ENTOURAGE OF HIS ROYAL HIGHNESS, FRANCIS III OF LORRAINE, VALENTIN JAMEREY-DUVAL BECAME FASCINATED BY WHAT HE SOON DISCOVERED THERE: "THE GARDENS FILLED ME WITH ADMIRATION BY THEIR DIVERSITY, THEIR VAST EXPANSES AND THE MAGNIFICENT REALISATION OF THEIR DISTRIBUTION." His admiration continued: "After the gushing waters and the foreign plants, what attracted my attention the most while navigating the gardens of Versailles was the prodigious number of statues of which they are inhabited." It was perhaps because he considered that "most of these statues are copied upon excellent models from Ancient Greece and Rome, and that modern sculptors could do no better than to imitate them" that he did not mention the *Milo of Croton* by Pierre Puget. It is true that this work had nothing in common with the sculptures of "Ancient Greece and Rome", which the students of the Academy of France in Rome (created by Louis XIV in 1666) regularly

Right:
*Puget presenting his
statue of Milo of Croton
to Louis XIV, in the
gardens of Versailles,*
Eugène Deveria, 1832.

copied with models that were scattered around the alleyways of Versailles. Puget's movement accompanied the Baroque style that was elaborated by Bernini in Rome for the service of the Catholic Church and its Counter-Reformation, which set about re-conquering what it saw as souls lost to Protestantism, just as supposedly it needed to convert others in the Americas and Asia.

COMPLETED IN MARSEILLES IN **1682,** Puget's sculpture arrived in Versailles during the summer of the following year. The work, commissioned by Colbert, met with the king's admiration. The athlete portrayed was all that could be expected. The fable has it that his exceptional force gave Milo his first victory at the Olympic Games of 540 BC, followed by success at five more of the events. Added to these were several wins at the

Below:
*View of the Green Carpet
at Versailles in 1775*
(in the foreground
are Louis XVI and
Marie-Antoinette),
Hubert Robert, 1775.

Pythian, Nemean and Isthmian games. It is also said that Milo, a disciple of Pythagoras, saved the philosopher when he alone held up the ceiling of a hall that was about to collapse, allowing the master and his audience to escape. But legend has it that, one day, he wanted to push open the trunk of an oak tree, broken in two. But his hands became trapped. Stuck at the spot, he was finally devoured by a lion. When the sculpture was presented before the court in the park of Versailles, at the entrance of the Royal Alley where it was judged to deserve its proper place, the queen, almost fainting, murmured: "The poor man, how he is suffering!"

MANY YEARS LATER, Louis XVI and Marie-Antoinette also appraised Puget's sculpture. But in the painting of the scene by Hubert Robert, it was not Milo's suffering that appears to concern them. Rather, it was the trees of the park that were toppled by a storm. It was neither the first nor the last time that the gardens suffered from the wrath of the weather. Saint -Simon recounted that, in 1701, came a "hurricane so furious" that "it [began] the epoch of seasonal disorder and the frequency of great winds in all seasons; cold at all times, rain etc., became much more ordinary since, and this bad weather has only increased until now to a point where it has been a long while since there have been springs, and there have been few autumns, and for summer, only a few days here and there. There is matter there to exercise astronomers."

SAINT-SIMON WROTE THAT LOUIS XIV pleased himself by tyrannising nature, to subdue it with the force of art and treasures." Was nature answering back to the monarch, sending him a message that it would not be con-tained by his power, however absolute it pretended to be? We do not know what the king thought of Fénelon's cutting observation: "Each one wants to have gardens where one digs up all the earth, with fountains, statues, parks without limits, and houses which demand an upkeep that surpasses the revenues of the land on which they stand. Where does all that come from? From the example of just one."

Opposite page:
The Milo of Croton,
Pierre Puget, 1683.

Garden of 'miracles'

THE COMPOSITION OF THE GARDENS OF VERSAILLES, WITH THEIR PARTERRES, THEIR FLOWER BANKS AND THEIR BOSQUETS AND GROVES, DEMANDED HIGHLY CAPABLE AND DEDICATED STAFF. They had quite remarkable skills, and their successes were the fruit of huge effort. The courtesan who accompanies the king on his walk around them could never imagine that, say, the hundreds of flowers just flowering on a bank in front of them actually came from the Americas, acclimatised in the Rochefort hothouses. Others come from the Mediterranean basin, and to ensure their safe and gradual transfer to northern climbs, Colbert aquired, in 1680, a garden of acclimatisation in the southern French port of Toulon. Seven years earlier, he ordered the intendant of the town of Caen, in Normandy, to do what was needed to deliver 10,000 daffodil bulbs to Versailles. He also asked the intendant of Marseille to organise delivery to Versailles of tuberoses from the Ottoman Empire and "all the other interesting flowers that you could think might contribute to the ornament." Later, he ordered roses from Provence for the gardens of Marly.

TREES ALSO CAME from many different places. Did Marly need holly? Then it was brought from Fontainebleau. Elms are needed for the lake? Some 6,000 were brought down to Versailles in 1680 from a forest near Compiègne. Eight years later, another 25,000 others were also delivered. Yew trees came from Normandy, maples from Montpellier, coniferous trees were brought from the eastern Dauphiné region. After all, there was no reason that the garden would present a greater challenge than the palace, for which marble and stone were transported from Italy, Flanders and the Pyrenees, from the Languedoc and England. In his *New description of the palaces and parks of Versailles and Marly*, published in 1723, Pignol de la Force wrote that Louis XIV had been "this great king [who] never tires of beautifying or nature or surpassing it." Charles Perrault dedicated the following verses to Versailles: "No, its rather a world where from the great universe / are found all together miracles quite diverse."*

Above:

A promenade by Louis XIV within view of the North parterre in the gardens of Versailles, around 1688, Etienne Allegrain.

PERHAPS IT WAS A GESTURE of loyalty towards his great-grandfather that Louis xv ordered the establishment of a botanical garden close to the Small Trianon. But the king probably only very rarely accompanied the gardener in charge of its many hothouses, Richard, or Bernard de Jussieu, who had just begun a detailed classification of the some 4,000 different plants found there.

"Dead leaves were never to be seen,
nor were shrubs that were not in flower."*
Le Nôtre

Above:

Louis-Philippe, his family and the Duchess of Kent take part in the Great Waters display at Versailles, May, 1844,
François-Edme Ricois, 1844.

The princely pleasures of peas and plums

MADAME DE SÉVIGNÉ REVEALED HOW PEAS WERE A MAJOR SUBJECT OF CONVERSATION AT VERSAILLES: "THE IMPATIENCE TO EAT THEM, THE PLEASURE TO HAVE EATEN THEM AND THE JOY AT EATING THEM AGAIN ARE THE THREE ISSUES WITH WHICH OUR PRINCES HAVE BEEN CONCERNED FOR THE LAST FEW DAYS. There are several ladies who, after having supped with the King, flaunt the risk of indigestion by retiring to their quarters with some peas to savour before going to bed. It is the fashion, it is all the rage." If the peas have sent the court into such a fever, then naturally they have come from the king's very own vegetable garden.

WHEN, IN 1673, JEAN-BAPTISTE LA QUINTINIE was named intendant of the king's fruit garden, it clearly had nothing to do with his experience as a lawyer with the court of the Paris parliament. It was more his knowledge of early written works about agronomy and, in particular, his field study of methods used in farms of the Roman countryside that allowed him, upon his return from that trip, to create the garden of the Hôtel Tambonneau in Paris. His innovative approach would soon establish his reputation. In 1678, by which time he had for eight years occupied the post of director of the fruit and vegetable gardens of all the royal households, he was given the task of transforming what was called "the stinking pond". He turned it into the King's Vegetable Garden.

THE METAMORPHOSIS was not a straightforward affair. The site needed draining, before it was filled with mud from what became, little by little, the Swiss Pond - and which was described as "of the sort that one would not want to find anywhere." A more fertile soil was brought by machine from the Satory hill. After that was put in place a stone network which "is a small water conduit set out below the earth with dry stone rubble underneath to drain subterranean water which would otherwise make the soil of the garden too damp, too cold and rotten." All this work created a large square area within which 16 vegetable patches were set out around a large, central water basin. The large square was finally surrounded with high walls to create 29 enclosed

Opposite page:
A view of the King's
Vegetable Garden.

Below, left:
Fruit from the King's
Vegetable Garden.
Below, right:
Decoration detail.
These fruit, represented
in the 18th, Century,
are probably modelled
on those from the King's
Vegetable Garden.

gardens in which other vegetables were grown, as well as, here and
there, fruit trees, some of them espaliered. Because this vegetable
garden is that of the king, who is present at Versailles, it also had to
be something of a theatre stage when it was at last completed, in
1683. Dominated by a terrace, it was indeed a spectacle worthy of
Louis the Great. La Quintinie defined the criteria for this: "It is necessary that one's eyes first of all find matter for pleasure, and that
there is nothing that is bizarre or hurtful; the most beautiful figure,
for a fruit orchard or a vegetable patch, is a fine square shape, especially when the corners are at right angles and that the length exceeds
one and a half, or two times, the extent of the width."

THE KING'S GARDENER HAD NO TIME for the almanacs of the time that suggested a gardener could "forecast the length of winter when he will see that oak trees will be abundant in their fruit, or that the duck has a reddened breast, or that the hornets appear before the end of October." He did not have faith either in the proverbs of Leduc, in 1664, which offered: "A year of snow / A fructuous year", "Never will rain in spring / Be called bad weather" or "Buds that show in April / See little wine for the barrel". The only one of Leduc's offerings that may have interested him was: "The almanac that gives us fear / Is most that which fools us most". No, La Quintinie was convinced by his own methods, such as the use of manure and glass cloches, which made it possible to supply figs, melons and strawberries to the kings table at all seasons. The king himself occasionally descended into the vegetable and fruit gardens, as the Marquis de Dangeau noted in his Journal for the date of August 31st, 1684: "The King walked around his gardens and his vegetable patches, where he allowed those who followed him to pick and eat fruit."

Above:
The Saint-Louis Cathedral, as seen from the King's Vegetable Garden.

La Quintinie died in 1687, one year after he was ennobled by the king. His disciples continued to scrupulously follow the directions set out in his *Instructions for the Fruit and Vegetable Gardens*. On December 28th, 1704, Madame wrote: "The king has no exotic fruit in his vegetable garden, but he has good local fruit. I have never seen raw pineapple, I have only seen preserves." She could have discovered what a pineapple looked like before it was turned into a preserve by descending the Staircase of One Hundred Steps, built between 1684 and 1686, to the orangery.

"The pleasure of seeing,
in the middle of snow and wintry
weather, an abundance of
asparagus, all plump, green and
really quite excellent, is enough to
remove any regrets about anything
else; and in truth it can be said
that it is only for the king to taste
this pleasure, and that it is perhaps
not the least that his Versailles
has produced for him, by the care
that I have the honour of taking."*
La Quintinie

Above:
A View of the Orangery, the One-Hundred Steps and the Palace of Versailles, around 1695, Jean-Baptiste Martin.

The marvel of Marly

SAINT-SIMON RECORDED THAT LOUIS XIV, "HAVING HAD ENOUGH OF THE BEAUTIFUL THINGS AND THE CROWD", SOUGHT SOMEWHERE NEAR TO VERSAILLES THAT WOULD SATISFY HIS NEED FOR SOLITUDE: "BEHIND LOUVECIENNES, HE FOUND A DEEP AND NARROW VALLEY, BORDERED BY STEEP BANKS, INACCESSIBLE BECAUSE OF ITS SWAMPS, WITHOUT ANY VIEW, CLOSED IN BY HILLS EVERYWHERE, VERY CRAMPED, WITH A NASTY LITTLE VILLAGE SET ON THE SLOPES OF ONE OF THESE HILLS AND THAT WAS CALLED MARLY." After the king's choice of Versailles, which Saint-Simon described as "the most sad and unprepossessing of all places, without a view, with no woods, no water, no land, because all was quicksand and marshland, and by consequence without any air", the king had showed in Marly a remarkable consistency. The duke sadly concluded: "Such was the King's bad taste in all things, and this pleasure in forcing nature, that neither the most trying war, nor devotion, could ever have the better of it." Despite it all, what was previously nothing more than a "place for snakes and carrions, for toads and frogs" was soon turned into the king's "hermitage."

THERE IS NO TRACE OF IT LEFT TODAY, apart from a drinking trough. The château, built by the architects Jules Hardouin-Mansart and Robert de Cotte between 1679 and 1684, was sold by the state in 1799 and transformed into a cotton mill and sheet factory. Some years later it was dismantled. Despite this banal end, Marly was one of the most important of the scenes-behind-the-scenes of Versailles.

IF, FOR A COURTESAN, to live at the court was a privilege, to be invited to Marly by the king was the privilege of all privileges. The Countess of Boigne was invited there during the last years of the reign of Louis XVI. "At Marly we were lodged, furnished and fed", she recalled. "Those invited to reside there were placed at various tables, headed by princes and princesses in their respective pavilions, at the King's expense." To be allowed to take a place at these tables, one had to accept the risk of being humiliated: "We had to register, that was how it was called, meaning that men and women went to see the First Gentleman of the room.

We wrote our names down in person, by hand; it was from this list that the choice of invitations were made, by eliminating those who should not have been asked, in such a way that a non-invitation carried with it the disgrace of refusal."* The strict rules of the proceedings remained the same since Louis XIV. It would certainly have been more humiliating still to have dared asked the king, "Sire, Marly?", and to have received nothing but silence in reply.

THE ETIQUETTE THAT REIGNED at Versailles, and regulated life there, was given leave at Marly. This disconcerted Madame, sister-in-law to Louis XIV, who wrote of her confusion in a letter dated August 2nd, 1705: "We no longer know who we are; when the King walks about, everyone covers themselves; if the Duchess of Burgundy goes for a walk, well, she gives her arm to a lady and the others walk beside them separately. You no longer

Above:
The machine of the Marly aqueduct, Pierre-Denis Martin.

recognise who she is."* Madame was gravely concerned: "I have great difficulty in getting used to this confusion; one cannot have an opinion because everything is at the present, all this no longer resembles a court."* In fact, it apparently resembled one so little that the behaviour of some would have been intolerable in Versailles. Already, on December 4th, 1695, Madame wrote: "The night before last at Marly there was a horrible dispute which made me laugh heartily. The Great Princess of Conti had reproached Mme de Chartres and Mme la duchesse for becoming drunk; she called them wine bags. To that the others replied that she was a sack of rubbish. Now, there's a princely dispute!"*

LOUIS XIV WAS EVEN MORE concerned about his garden in Marly than he was about that of Versailles. Dangeau recorded that one day "he amused himself by having the trees pruned", and that on another "he gave orders for several little things he wanted done here to his cascade and his fountains."* In Marly, because it was impossible to do so in Versailles, the king could ask for the water displays to function all day.

IF MARLY WAS A PRIVELEGED WING of the court, it was also a privileged site among all the gardens, and fundamental to them all. It was at Marly that was erected the formidable machine that, from 1681, made it possible for water to arrive in Versailles. It was in 1679 that the king gave Colbert and Mansart the task of finding, in consultation with learned engineers, how to bring waters from the river Seine, which ran below the hills of Louveciennes, to the top of the hill and then on to the necessary reservoirs via an aqueduct. Mansart told the king: "I will tomorrow enquire of France's learned ones, and the water will [even] be carried right up to the sky, if it so pleases your Majesty."*

AFTER PROVING IN FRONT OF THE KING that the machine he had conceived was capable of bringing the waters of the Seine from the Palfour mill right up to the terraces of the château of Saint-Germain, Arnold de Ville was given the task of building the machine at Marly. Some believed that Rennequin Sualem, who at the time of his death on July 29th, 1707 was the master carpenter in charge of the machine's maintenance, would have had the necessary experience to build such a machine, having been involved with a similar one in a mine near Liège. Whatever, in his *Memoirs to serve the history of Louis XIV*, the Abbot of Choisy wrote: "Eight thousand francs as a pension for M. de Ville, a gentleman from Liège, who invented and carried to perfection the machine of Marly. No-one begrudged him such a sum; it thanks to him that we have such wonderful waters in Versailles. This machine is admirable for both its grandeur and at the same time for its simplicity."*

A FEW YEARS BEFORE "In Marly, one does not have an apartment, except for sleeping and dressing; but once this is done, everything is public. In the King's apartment, there is music; in that of the dauphin, meals are consumed, as much at midday as in the evening; that's also where the billiard is, which is always crowded."

"In Marly, one does not have an apartment, except for sleeping and dressing; but once this is done, everything is public. In the King's apartment, there is music; in that of the dauphin, meals are consumed, as much at midday as in the evening; that's also where the billiard is, which is always crowded."*
Madame, duchess of Orleans, née Princess Palatine

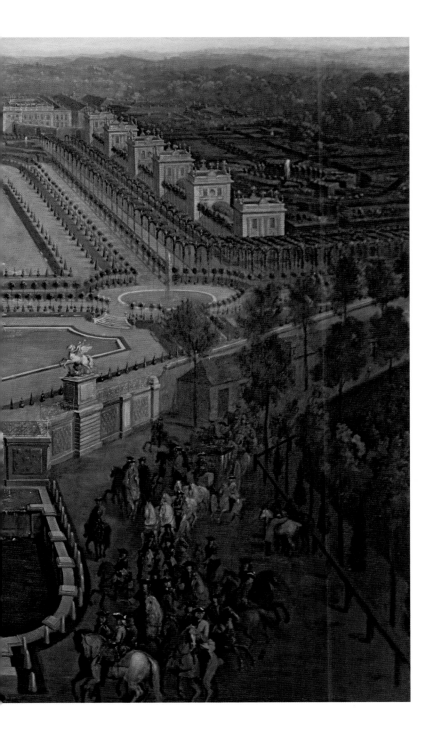

Left:
Château de Marly,
F. Prudhomme, *1922,*
after P.D. Martin,
circa 1722.

The guardians of austerity and the Garden of Eden

THE OPERA *PROLOGUE D'ALCESTE,* OR *THE TRIOMPH OF ALCIDES,* BY JEAN-BAPTISTE LULLY AND PHILIPPE QUINAULT, WAS REHEARSED IN THE APARTMENT OF MADAME DE MONTESPAN AT THE END OF 1673 BEFORE IT WAS PERFORMED IN THE MARBLE COURTYARD OF THE PALACE OF VERSAILLES IN JULY 1674 AS PART OF FESTIVITIES CELEBRATING THE CONQUEST OF THE FRANCHE-COMTÉ. In the prologue, these verses are sung: "Art in accord with nature / Serves love in these charming places / These waters that make on dream by such a soft murmur / These carpets where flowers form so many ornaments / These lawns, these beds of green / All is created but for lovers."* They were a prefect introduction to what would be played out over a long period of time on the other side of the palace, in the gardens...

THE DUCHESS OF RETZ more than anyone, had wanted this invitation would become a reality. Without shame, she had herself called 'Madame of Give-It-To-Me'. He husband tried in vain to bring her round to more decency. To rid herself of migraines and insomnia, she maintained there was no better remedy than to go back and forth naked among the bosquets in the garden and to make love with... Whether he who meets her and wraps together with her is a gentleman, valet, page or musketeer has strictly no importance. 'Madame of Give-it-to-Me' was the exact opposite of 'Madame Etiquette'. That was the nickname given to the Countess of Noailles, a very upright and severe woman, by the dauphiness Marie-Antoinette of Austria, whose final years of education were entrusted to the Countess.

IN HER *MEMOIRS OF THE PRIVATE LIFE OF MARIE-ANTOINETTE,* Madame Campan noted that "the queen should have had a lady-in-waiting who gave her full instruction on the origin of these etiquettes, in reality most bothersome but erected like an imposing barrier against malevolence." Her choice of listening "more to gibes than to reason" had fatal consequences. Because she would not take heed of 'Madame Etiquette', she would soon find herself considered as another 'Madame Give-It-To-Me'.

This nickname is no worse than those that would be sang in the street before the queen was labelled as 'The Austrian', or 'Madame Deficit', or even 'Madame Veto'. During her trial in 1793, the debauchery of which she was suspected for some years led Jacques-René Hébert to accuse her of incest. When a juror questioned her silence, Marie-Antoinette stood up and said: "If I did not answer it is because nature itself refuses to answer such an accusation made against a mother. For this, I call upon all those who are here today!"

WAS THE SMALL TRIANON THE FIRST TO ACCUSE HER? For the Marquis de Bombelles, it was built for love: "The Small Trianon is surrounded by all pleasantness that nature can offer. The small mounds of its gardens are covered with flowers and all the various trees of the four quarters of the world. Well-designed paths lead to a Temple of Love. Its statue in white marble is a quite marvellous copy of the excellent original by

Above:
The Temple of Love, with the Small Trianon in the background. The sculpture of Love is a copy by L-P. Mouchy, based on the original by Edmé Bouchardon.

Bouchardon. The temple is not at all obscured by surrounding walls; elegant columns support the cupola, and, because Love is the most celebrated of all the gods of the fable, one can arrive from all sides to the foot of his alter."

AT VERSAILLES,, it was as if the nicknames that were first used in the behind-the-scenes world of the wings and corridors designated two distinct gardens: 'Madame Etiquette' is given the rigour of the parterres à la française that speak only of power. When the gardens begin to evoke only of love, power no longer imposes itself. The first garden,

then, commands respect. The second holds surprises. One only toler-
ates order. The other awaits a troubling emotion and pleasure. On the
subject of the decapitated queen, the Count of Ségur wrote: "It was
imprudent to listen only to her heart."

**Above
and opposite page:**
The Queen's Hamlet
is set in circular arcs
composing various
buildings and thatched
houses around an
artificial lake; this
was dominated by
a lighthouse, the
Malborough Tower,
built in 1786, notable
because it was related
to a performance by
the dauphin's nanny
of a song in *The Barber
of Seville.*

Opposite:
Series of drawings representing the buildings of the hamlet of the Small Trianon, John-Claude Nattes, circa 1802.

The secrets of the Small Trianon

IN **1802**, WITHIN AN INTERVAL OF A FEW MONTHS, TWO BRITONS MADE SEPARATE 'TOURIST' VISITS TO VERSAILLES, AN ADJECTIVE THAT HAD ONLY ENTERED THE FRENCH LANGUAGE SINCE SOME TWO YEARS. The first who arrived wrote to one of his friends: "We have dined at the Small Trianon, and also slept there. The bedroom that I had was also that of the unfortunate Louis XVI, and the key to the door was attached with a label upon which it was still possible to read, although well-worn, the words 'Appartement du Roi'."* The second tourist, arriving five months later, wrote: "The palace itself is now occupied by a caterer, and we dined in the former boudoir of the Queen, a small room adjoined to her bedchamber. All the furniture has gone and, of the former palace, there remains only its name. But all of this is very pretty."* While they both appeared pleased with their stay, the first noted tourist that he received a bill "so exorbitant that I kept it as something of interest."

THE WELL-WORN KEY label for the 'Appartements du Roi' no doubt justified the price asked for. To sleep in the room that belonged to a king can only be considered a privilege, and never comes cheaply. If the British guest had ever thought necessary to point out that Louis XVI in fact did not have an apartment in the Small Trianon, the room-keeper would have no doubt told him that he must have mistaken the words on the almost unreadable key tag; Louis XVI probably read: Louis XV.

AND THE HOTEL-KEEPER COULD have raised his price further if he had opened a trap-door. But no doubt it was too-well hidden. It at one time allowed the elevation from the kitchen of a ready-dressed table before which Louis XV was ready to dine with Madame du Barry or, at a later period, perhaps Marie-Antoinette accompanied by Madame de Lamballe, the Duke of Coigny, the Count of Guines and the Baron of Besenval, to whom her favour was a source of irritation for the court. The court was also annoyed by the favour she accorded to the two 'Jules' – Jules de Polignac and Jules de Vaudreuil. The room-keeper might also have let his

Above:
The Small Trianon, from the garden.

British guest understand that if such a particular contraption had been built, it was because each of them was 'dressed', if the word is not too inappropriate, for the occasion of its use.

THE LIBERTINE, OR EVEN RIBALD, sous-entendus could have continued with a visit to another other bedroom whereby a device allowed mirrors to close before the windows, thereby avoiding any indiscrete attention. It was quite probable, however, that by that time the mirrors had been stolen.

Below, left:
The system of mirror flaps in one of the rooms of the Small Trianon.
Below, right:
The lift shaft by which a dressed table was sent unaccompanied from the kitchens to the private apartments.

WITH THE DISAPPEARANCE of the hidden tables and mirrors, the Revolution deprived at least one tradesman of Versailles from an honest living with what would no doubt have been a fruitful commerce with tourists.

"One must visit
        this magical palace,
Where there are wonderful verses,
        dance and music,
With the art of confusing eyes
        with colours,
And the more pleasant art
        of seducing hearts,
Where one, unique pleasure is had
        From one hundred others."*

Voltaire

Preceding page
Top: Bedroom of mirrors.
Bottom: Hidden staircase.

Above:
The Small Trianon from the courtyard.

Playing a part

She had first learned how to play comedy, to sing and to play music, in the Austrian capital Vienna. That was also how she began learning the French language. So it was, that on June 1ˢᵗ, 1780, Marie-Antoinette's dearest wish was finally granted when she took to the stage of her own small theatre in Versailles, which was completed the previous year. The stage was larger than either the seating area or the orchestra pit, which could contain about 20 musicians. She felt reassured that, along with the comedies and tragedies that could be represented there, operas could also be performed. She was soon continually busy learning roles, rehearsing and taking to the stage. The Count Florimond de Mercy-Argenteau, who venerated her mother, the Empress Maria Theresa of Austria, was quick to tell the latter that rehearsals and representations lasted quite some time, and that they were followed by "a supper restricted to members of the royal family and the actors and actresses." This was something that soon irritated the court. The Duke of Fronsac, disturbed that he had not been invited to one of her performances, was told by the queen that the requirements of etiquette did not have their place at Trianon: "[...] I do not hold court there; I live as an individual."

She presented plays by Favart and Sedaine, operas by Grétry and Gluck. She herself sang one of the roles in Jean-Jacques Rousseau's opera *Le Devin du Village (The Village Soothsayer).* That the queen Maria Leszczynska, who preceded her on the French throne, sourly regretted that the author did not restrict himself to such works did not trouble Marie-Antoinette. But others were disturbed when she chose to stage, on February 23ʳᵈ, 1775, *The Barber of Seville* by Pierre-Augustin Caron de Beaumarchais, which was first performed 10 years earlier. When that turned out to be a flop, the queen turned to the latest work completed by Beaumarchais, *The Marriage of Figaro*, which had met with great success since its first public performance on April 27ᵗʰ, 1784; even those concerned by the seditious words it contained had flocked to the 68 triumphal presentations that followed.

Opposite page
Top: The Queen's Small Theatre, in the Small Trianon.
Bottom: A detail from the decoration of the stage curtain.

How could the queen choose to perform works by such a scandalous author and even play, herself, the role of Rosine? Perhaps she found pleasure in mocking the court when, in Scene I of Act II, she pronounced the words "I don't know if these walls have eye and ears". One can imagine how the backstage world of Versailles appeared designated when she sends Figaro on his way with "Leave by the harpsichord room, and descend as softly as you can" or, a few scenes later, she tells him to

Preceding double page, from top left, clockwise: The ceiling as seen from the prompter's box. The flies of the Queen's Theatre. Under the stage. The steps from the prompter's box.
Below: The arbour leading to the Queen's Hamlet.

"leave by the little stairway." After the performance, one can imagine her sitting in the garden of the Hamlet nearby, singing her part in Scene IV, Act III: "The sighs / The attentions, the promises / The lively tenderness / The Pleasures / The subtle banter / Are put to use / And soon the shepherdess / No longer feels anger." It was to avoid the anger caused to her by the constraints of etiquette that she had asked for the theatre to be built, just like the farm, the cow sheds, the barn, the henhouse and the dairy…

WHEN, AFTER HER ARREST FOLLOWING THE REVOLUTION, she was transferred from the Temple to the Conciergerie, one can but wonder if she remembered the words of her part, addressing Bartholo in Scene IV, of Act II: "From a prison to a dungeon, the difference is so small!" Or maybe she regretted not taking the time, when she arrived on the throne at the age of 19, not having better learnt the role of queen?

"Because you're a great Nobleman you think you are a a great genius!… Nobility, riches, rank, position; all that makes one so proud! What have you done to acquire so much? You simply took the trouble of being born, nothing else. For the rest, you're rather an ordinary man!"*
Beaumarchais, *The Marriage of Figaro*, Act V, Scene III.

Vue perspective de la Grande et petite Ecurie, et des deux Cour

A Paris chez Jacques Chereau rue S.ᵗ Jacques, au dessus de la Fontaine S.ᵗ Se

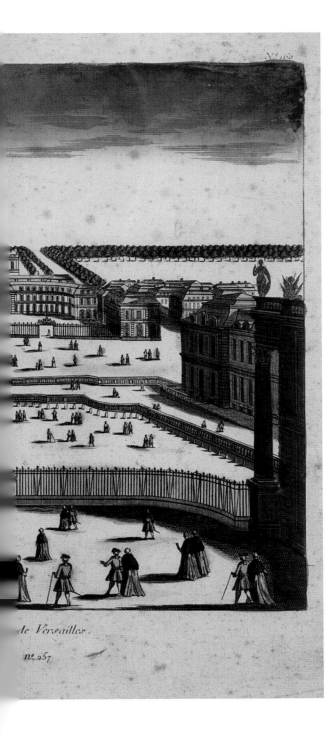

de Versailles.

nt. 257

Left:
*View from the Marble Courtyard towards
the Grand and Small Stables,* 1650.

Stable events

SITUATED IN FRONT OF THE PALACE, AT THE BACK OF THE PLACE D'ARMES, THE GRAND AND SMALL STABLES ACTUALLY HAVE THE SAME DIMENSIONS. The 'grandness' of one, and the 'smallness' of the other, is in fact a description of their roles. The Grand Stable houses riding horses, while the symmetrical Small Stable is for draught horses. To build them, Hardouin-Mansart destroyed in 1680 the residential mansions, called 'hôtels', of the Lauzun, de Noailles and Guitry families which stood between the three avenues at the point where they converge onto the large square.

THE ROYAL EQUERRY, who etiquette demanded should be called Monsieur le Grand, was in charge of ensuring the king was supplied with all the horses that he needed for military campaigns and for hunting, choosing the appropriate stallions, managing the school for pages and the stud farm, as well as delegating tasks to the harbingers, the officers and the coachmen — and yet more still. Very soon after the stables were completed, he had to deal with a quite unexpected event. Philippe Quinault's five-act lyric tragedy *Perseus*, with music by Jean-Baptiste Lully, had recently opened in Paris (in April 1682) and was to be given an outdoors performance in Versailles. For the *Prologue*, Quinault directed: "The theatre stage represents a bocage." But rain threatened on the night of the performance.

WITHIN A FEW HOURS, everything was put in place in the Grand Stable. The *Mercure français* reported: "Theatre, orchestra, the high canopy, nothing was missing. A very large number orange trees, of quite extraordinary width and which were very difficult to move about and even more difficult to mount upon the stage, found themselves placed there. All at the rear was leaves, composed of veritable branches and greenery cut from the forest. At the back and among the orange trees there were a quantity of figures of fauns and divinities, and a large number of girandoles. Many people who knew what this place looked like a few hours before found it hard to believe what they saw." It would, of course, have been inconceiv-

Opposite page:
The stables of Versailles, transformed for the Bartabas equestrian academy.

able to make the king wait. In the *Prologue*, the character that is Phronime sings: "Virtue wants to choose this place to retire to." Indeed, it would have been just as unthinkable to keep Virtue waiting.

ON DECEMBER 15TH, 1751, the Grand Stable was the stage of a quite different spectacle. Louis xv had granted permission to the people of Versailles to hold a firework display that day in celebration of the birth, on December 13ᵗʰ, of a son to the dauphin and his second wife, Maria-Josepha of Saxony. But the festivities were soured when a rocket fell through a skylight window on the roof, setting fire to the forage of hay and straw that filled the attic. Immediately, the French and Swiss guards

Below:
The school of the Bartabas equestrian academy.

were mobilised and every possible pump was set to work. But after the fire was brought under control three hours later, nothing was left of the roofing or the timber framework. There was irony in that Sully's tragedy, played there in 1682, contained the lines: "Gods punish pride / There is no grandeur that an irritated sky / cannot lower when it wants, and reduce to powder."*

Above:
The courtyard
of the Grand Stables.
The three horses in the
tympanum above the
door are the work of
Garnier and Raon.

Imagination

The Revolution had passed when the poet Jacques Delille returned to Versailles. It had nothing in common with that for which he had written, *The Gardens*, in **1782**. *The Imaginations*, written 20 years later, were nothing more than nostalgia: "See these deserted walls / There the pompous Versailles / Once spread the arrogance of its walls: / There a thousand passions, a thousand wishes altogether / The Princes and the grand ones, the representatives of the Kings, / The rival interests, the misleading vanities, / Unceasingly cavorted on these pompous roads; / There, came in silence, waiting for a glance of the eye, / Unto the feet of favour knelt pride / From there, carried far away on the Earth and on waves, / The will of one alone decided the fate of the world. / Such a brilliant display irritated a dazzled universe; / A storm thundered, and everything disappeared!"* But the power of the palace to fascinate continued. The Viscount François-René de Chateaubriand wrote: "This palace, which itself is like a large town, these marble staircases that seem to climb up to the skies, these statues, these basins, these woods, are now crumbling, or covered with moss, or dried out, or knocked down, and yet this residence of kings has never appeared more pompous, nor less solitary."*

After the signing of the Treaty of Amiens in 1802, the British were once again able to visit France. Like those of them who had travelled to Versailles a few years earlier for the auction of palace furniture that began on June 19th, 1794, the British in general never ceased to be fascinated by the place that became, as of 1797, the seat of a special museum of the French School. One of the first to return, in April, 1802, was called J. G. Lemaistre, a writer who hailed from the Scottish capital Edinburgh. In one of his regular letters to a friend, he wrote: "This magnificent edifice did not at all suffer during the Revolution. However, following a lack of maintenance and being no longer inhabited, it has a character of sadness that can only remind one of the misfortunes of its last owners and the fragility of human grandeur."

Above:
View of the palace as seen from the heights of Satory, A. F. Van der Meulen, 1664.

Sir John Dean Paul undertook the same journey. In his *Diary of a Journey to Paris* in August 1802 he noted: "[...] crossing the great courtyard of the palace, our eyes could only see, on all sides, pillage and devastation. This façade of the palace, although imposing and architecturally rich, is less pretty than the other. But who could without emotion contemplate these broken and now bricked-up windows, these doors falling off their hinges, the grass covering the courtyard cobbles, at the very same spot where previously the slightest blade would have been removed, and where every-thing was splendour and gaiety. The edifice was very badly damaged to its exterior; all the royal emblems have been scratched out; several cornices have been damaged by guns, and all over there hangs a feeling of ruin to come. We cross the magnificent halls where paintings of no inter-est have been left, while the best have been removed. The mirrors have been carried away and the frames left empty. Although almost all the furniture has been removed, these apartments still keep an aspect of grandeur that impresses one."*

Some years later, Austrian Emperor Francis I sent special envoy Charles de Clary-et-Aldringen to France with the mission of delivering by hand a let-ter to Napoleon, who had become the emperor's son-in-law since his marriage to Marie-Louise in Vienna on March 11th, 1810. Charles de Clary-et-Aldringen could not avoid visiting Versailles, a model for the Schönbrunn Palace, and recounted the experience in a letter. The pal-ace, he wrote, "is in a pitiful state of degradation, not one piece of fur-niture, nothing but paintings from the new French school. The old ceil-ing paintings are peeling, the mirrors are broken. Each door, each window recalls some event. There are, on the one side, the memories of Louis xiv, and on the other those of the Revolution, and they so con-fuse what was the highest glory of the throne and its greatest lowness that one can hardly tell them apart." In the same letter, he recounted his journey from Paris to Versailles: "Already on the road I thought I saw it covered in carriages, people coming and going, courtesans seeking to be

Above:
The Parterre d'Eau at Versailles, Richard Parkes Bonington, 1826.

noticed, for a word from the master. I saw this grand golden carriage of Louis XIV, I saw him himself, with his great locks and small hat, heady with incense, able to believe himself King of the World, surrounded by guards, followed by all the court; I saw, in the third carriage, Mlle de la Vallière...Imagination! But how can one not have it here, where everything speaks of the past?"*

IT WAS NO COINCIDENCE that the poet Delille, writing of the same palace, entitled his poem *The Imaginations*, and this Austrian aristocrat who gives an exclamation mark to the word 'Imagination'. Versailles had been the seat of absolute power, and it was there that this power had become absolutely contested. For centuries, it was the stage of every intrigue; that is why it continues to excite imagination. And in the behind-the-scenes world of this palace where everything was a stage wing, imagination offers history its clothes.

WHEN IMAGINATION TAKES HOLD of history's attributes, this becomes 'restoration' in the language of museums. But the imagination of those who visit Versailles is not bothered about the detail that concerned the restorers, such as replacing the balusters of the Gabriel Staircase at vertical, instead of perpendicular angle to the flight of the stairs. Nor whether the parquet flooring of the Hall of Mirrors had to be repaired after World War II, or that the torchères are in resin. Nor, again, that the Royal Gate, was put back with its fixations attached to the Dufour Pavilion, built under the Second Empire, and which did not exist when the gate was ripped away during the Revolution for the sans-culottes to make spikes out of. The list is endless because Versailles never ceased, nor ceases to be, a permanent building site.

"Oh Versailles, oh woods, oh porticos,
      Living marbles, ancient bowers,
Elysium adorned by gods and kings,
      To your countenance, in my thoughts,
Like cool dew on parched grass,
      A little calm and oblivion flows.

The chariots, the royal wonders
      The nocturnal watch of guards,
All has fled; of grandeurs you are no longer
          the keeper:
      But sleep, solitude,
Gods before never known, the arts
      and reflection
      Today compose your court."*

André Chénier

Post-Scriptum & Acknowledgments

Besides this image of one of the confessionals in the sacristy of palace chapel — where one can only guess who could have repented and for what sin (s) — the author confesses... He knows only too well that he could not have recounted everything about Versailles and its world 'behind the scenes'. How could he have had such an idea? He had to leave out this place and that, and to leave some events unmentioned. He realises that, in the end, these pages can only be an introduction. His wish is to have, through something of an after-taste of frustration that they may have left, encouraged readers to (re) discover Versailles in a different manner.

The publisher and the author express their thanks to Monsieur Jean-Jacques Aillagon, President of the Public Establishment of the museum and national domain of Versailles, for the welcome and interest he gave to this book when it was still but a project, and to Monsieur Jean-Vincent Bacquart for his attention and help. They similarly thank Madame Jeanne Hollande for having allowed Gilles Targat privileged access to the palace and its 'backstage' areas, and this in the best conditions; and among those accompanying him, Monsieur Jean-Jannick Mussard, who showed great kindness and efficiency while opening the doors of this labyrinth.

They would also like to thank Madame Béatrice Kleinert-Nicolas for having allowed the photography, in her restoration workshop, of the copies executed by Prudhomme, between 1920 and 1922, of paintings of P.D. Martin representing the Palace of Versailles and the Château of Marly. They are grateful to her also for having obtained permission for their reproduction here from the owners of the paintings, who they also thank.

A (very) short Bibliography

This bibliography does not list either guidebooks or sources such as
Memoirs and other texts and works of the C17th and C18th;
Those it mentions are recent titles that incite a discovery of Versailles
in all its different forms and which inspire further (varied) reading...

Baraton (Alain), *Le Jardinier de Versailles*, Grasset, Paris, 2006;
Barry (Joseph), *Versailles: Passions and Politics of an Era*, Littlehampton
Book Services Ltd, 1972;
Levron (Jacques), *Les inconnus de Versailles*, Perrin, Paris, 2003;
La Vie quotidienne à la cour de Versailles aux VIIᵉ et XVIIIᵉ siècles,
Hachette, Paris,1965;
Lenôtre (G.), *Versailles au temps des Rois*, Les Cahiers rouges (coll.),
Grasset, Paris, 1995;
Ritchey Newton (William), *Derrière la façade, Vivre au château de Versailles au
XVIIIᵉ siècle*, Perrin, Paris, 2008;
Saule (Béatrix), *Versailles triomphant, une journée de Louis XIV*, Flammarion,
Paris, 1996;
Solnon (Jean-François), *Histoire de Versailles*, Tempus (coll.),
Perrin, Paris, 2003;
Tiberghien (Frédéric), Versailles, *Le chantier de Louis XIV, 1662-1715*,
Pour l'histoire (coll.), Perrin, Paris, 2002.

Index of names

Index of art works & photographic credits

p. 126-127: © RMN/ Michèle Bellot
View of the Royal Courtyard of the Château
de Versailles, Israël Silvestre, 1685, pen and ink watercolour,
Louvre, Paris.
p. 128: © AKG-images/Erich Lessing
Portrait of Madame de Maintenon, French School, 1680,
oil on canvas, Château de Bussy-Rabutin.
p. 132-133: © AKG-images/Archives CDA/Guillo
The Grand and Small Stables as seen from the Palace
circa 1690, oil on canvas, Châteaux de Versailles
et de Trianon.
p. 135: © RMN/Gérard Blot
Madame de la Vallière (Louise-Françoise de la Baume-
le-Blanc, represented as in the company of Diana), after
Claude Lefebvre, C17th, oil on canvas, Châteaux de Versailles
et de Trianon.
p. 137: © AKG-images
Marquise de Montespan, mistress of Louis XIV, after Pierre
Mignard, vers 1694, oil on canvas, Châteaux de Versailles
et de Trianon.
p. 138: © MBA, Rennes, Dist RMN/Adélaïde Beaudouin
Mademoiselle de la Vallière and her children, Sir Peter Lely,
C17th, oil on canvas, Rennes, Musée des Beaux-Arts.
p. 139: © RMN/Jean Popovitch
Madame de Montespan, the Duke of the Maine, the Count of
Vexin, Mademoiselle de Nantes et Mademoiselle de Tours,
after Pierre Mignard, C17th, oil on canvas, Châteaux
de Versailles et de Trianon.
p. 141: © RMN/Gérard Blot
"Sincerity": Ladies of the court and abbot of the court, in
front of a mirror, Henri Bonnart, C17th, print engraving,
Châteaux de Versailles et de Trianon.
p. 145: © AKG-images
Portrait of Madame de Pompadour, François Boucher, 1750,
oil on canvas, Waddesdon Manor, coll. Rothschild.
p. 146: © AKG-images
Portrait of Madame de Pompadour, Jean-Marc Nattier, 1748,
oil on canvas, Musée de l'Hôtel Sandelin, Saint-Omer.
p. 151: © Gilles Targat
p. 152-153: © Gilles Targat
p. 155: © AKG-images/Erich Lessing
Louis XVI giving instructions to La Pérouse, Nicolas Monsiau,
1817, oil on canvas, Châteaux de Versailles et de Trianon.
p. 156-157 : © AKG-images
An aerostatic experiment held at Versailles, September 19th,
copper engraving, Paris.
p. 158: © RMN/Gérard Blot/Hervé Lewandowski
The King gives orders for a simultaneous attack on four
Dutch fortified towns, 1672, on the ceiling of the Hall of
Mirrors, Charles Le Brun, 1680 to 1684, oil on canvas
marouflée, Châteaux de Versailles et de Trianon.
p. 160: ©RMN/Gérard Blot
Members of the royal family of France together with the
dauphin born in 1781, C18th, oil on canvas, Châteaux de
Versailles et de Trianon.
p. 161: © RMN/Gérard Blot
The children of France swept by Glory, Jean-François
de Troy, 1735, oil on canvas, Châteaux de Versailles et
de Trianon.
p. 162-163: © AKG-images
Meeting of the Estates-General at Versailles, May 5th, 1789,
Auguste Couder, 1839, oil on canvas, Châteaux de
Versailles et de Trianon.
p. 164: © Gilles Targat
p. 165: © AKG-images/Erich Lessing
Marie-Antoinette, surrounded by her court, playing
the pedal harp for her friends in her music room
in Versailles, 1777, oil on canvas, Châteaux de Versailles
et de Trianon.
p. 166-167: © Musée Lambinet
The Gentlemen of the Third Estate at the session
of June 23rd, 1789, Lucien Melingue, 1874,
Musée Lambinet, Versailles.
p. 168-169: © Gilles Targat

p. 170-171: © RMN/DR
Preparatory drawings for the Oath of the Jeu de Paume,
Jacques-Louis David, Châteaux de Versailles et de Trianon.
p. 172-173: © RMN/DR
Louis-Philippe is presented with the members of
the diplomatic corps in the Hall of Battles, during the
inauguration of the Versailles museum, June 10th, 1837,
François-Joseph Heim, C19th, oil on canvas, Châteaux
de Versailles et de Trianon.
p. 177: ©RMN/DR
Procession of Crusaders around Jerusalem, led by Pierre
l'Ermite and Godefroy de Bouillon, the day before the attack
on the town, July 14th, 1099, Jean-Victor Schnetz, 1841,
oil on canvas, Châteaux de Versailles et de Trianon.
p. 178: © RMN/DR
Louis-Philippe, the royal family and king Leopold 1st visiting
the Hall of Crusades of the palace of Versailles, in July 1844,
Prosper Lafaye, C19th, oil on canvas, Châteaux de Versailles
et de Trianon.
p. 178-179: © Gilles Targat
p. 180 et 181: © Gilles Targat
p. 182-183: © Gilles Targat
p. 184-185: © Gilles Targat
p. 186: © RMN/Gérard Blot
View of the labyrinth with Diana and her nymphs,
Jean Cotelle, C17th, oil on canvas, Châteaux de Versailles et
de Trianon.
p. 187: © AKG-images/CDA/Guillemot
View of the Arch of Triumph and of France triumphant
with nymphs enchaining captives before Mars and Venus,
Jean Cotelle, 1688, gouache, Châteaux de Versailles
et de Trianon.
p. 188 top, left: © RMN/Gérard Blot
View of the bosket and water theatre, or stage, with nymphs
preparing to receive Psyche, Jean Cotelle, 1688,
oil on canvas, Châteaux de Versailles et de Trianon.
Top, right: © RMN/Gérard Blot
View of the Dragon Pool and the ramp of the Neptune Pool
with Apollo killing the serpent Python, Jean Cotelle, C17th, oil
on canvas, Châteaux de Versailles et de Trianon.
p. 188 bottom: © AKG-images/CDA/Guillemot
View of the colonnade with Apollo and the nymphs, Jean
Cotelle, circa 1688, gouache, Châteaux de Versailles
et de Trianon.
Bottom, right: © AKG-images/CDA/Guillemot
View of the labyrinth with Diana and her nymphs,
Jean Cotelle, after 1688, gouache, Châteaux de Versailles
et de Trianon.
p. 189 left: © AKG-images/CDA/Guillemot
View of the Arch of Triumph, with Venus welcoming Mars,
Jean Cotelle, 1688, gouache, Châteaux de Versailles
et de Trianon.
p. 189 right: © AKG-images/CDA/Guillemot
A perspective of the Three-Fountains, Jean Cotelle, 1688,
gouache, Châteaux de Versailles et de Trianon.
p. 191: © RMN/Hervé Lewandowski
Louis XIV followed by the grand dauphin passing on
horseback before the Grotto of Thesis, circa 1684,
oil on canvas, Châteaux de Versailles et de Trianon.
p. 193: © RMN/DR
The project plan for the bosket of the Grotto of Apollo in
the gardens of Versailles, Hubert Robert, 1775, drawing,
Châteaux de Versailles et de Trianon.
p. 194-195: © AKG-images
View of the Palace of Versailles from a water parterre,
Perelle, 1670, copper engraving.
p. 197: © Gilles Targat
p. 198 left: © Gilles Targat
Right: © AKG-images/Erich Lessing
Portrait of André Le Nôtre, the architect who organised
the gardens of Versailles, Carlo Maratta, 1680,
oil on canvas, Châteaux de Versailles et de Trianon.
p. 199 top: © Gilles Targat
Bottom: © Gilles Targat

p. 200 left: © AKG-images/Erich Lessing
Puget presenting his statue of Milo of Croton to Louis XIV
in the gardens of Versailles, Eugène Deveria, 1832, painted
plaster, Musée du Louvre, Paris.
p. 201: © Gilles Targat
View of the Green Carpet at Versailles in 1775
(in the foreground are Louis XVI and Marie-Antoinette),
Hubert Robert, 1775, oil on canvas, Châteaux de Versailles
et de Trianon.
p. 203:© RMN
The Milo of Croton, Pierre Puget, 1683
p. 204-205: © RMN/Gérard Blot
A promenade by Louis XIV within view of the North parterre
in the gardens of Versailles, around 1688, Etienne Allegrain,
C17th, oil on canvas, Châteaux de Versailles et de Trianon.
p. 207-208: ©RMN/DR
Louis-Philippe, his family and the Duchess of Kent take
part in the Great Waters display at Versailles, May, 1844,
François-Edme Ricois, 1844, oil on canvas, Châteaux
de Versailles et de Trianon.
p. 208: © Gilles Targat
p. 210 left: © Gilles Targat
Right: © Gilles Targat
p. 211: © Gilles Targat
p. 212-213: © RMN/Franck Raux
A View of the Orangery, the One-Hundred Steps and the
Palace of Versailles, around 1695, Jean-Baptiste Martin,
C17th, oil on canvas, Châteaux de Versailles et de Trianon.
p. 215: © RMN/DR
The machine of the Marly aqueduct, Pierre-Denis Martin,
1C17th, oil on canvas, Châteaux de Versailles et de Trianon.
p. 218-219: © Gilles Targat
Château de Marly, F. Prudhomme 1922, after P.D. Martin
circa 1722, oil on canvas.
p. 221: © Gilles Targat
p. 222 et 223: © Gilles Targat
p. 224-225: © RMN/Gérard Blot
Series of drawings representing the buildings of the hamlet
of the Small Trianon, John-Claude Nattes, circa 1802, black
chalk and quill, Châteaux de Versailles et de Trianon.
p. 226-227: © Gilles Targat
p. 228: © Gilles Targat
Page 229 top: © Gilles Targat
Bottom: © Gilles Targat
p. 231 : © Gilles Targat
p. 233 top: © Gilles Targat
Bottom: © Gilles Targat
p. 234 top: © Gilles Targat
Bottom: © Gilles Targat
p. 235 top: © Gilles Targat
Bottom: © Gilles Targat
p. 236: © Gilles Targat
p. 238-239: © AKG-images/Archives CDA/ Guillo
View from the Marble Courtyard towards the Grand and
Small Stables, 1650, copper engraving.
p. 240: © Gilles Targat
p. 242: © Gilles Targat
p. 243: © Gilles Targat
p. 244-245: © AKG-images/Jérôme da Cunha
View of the palace as seen from the heights of Satory,
by A. F. Van der Meulen, oil on canvas, 1664,
Château de Versailles.
p. 246-247: © RMN/Gérard Blot
Le parterre d'eau à Versailles, Richard Parkes Bonington,
circa 1826, oil on canvas, Musée du Louvre, Paris.
p. 250: © Gilles Targat

Editor: Volcy Loustau
Art director: Gaëlle Junius
Translation: George Tanner
Realisation: Else

Production: Colombe Lecoufle
Photoengraving: Couleurs d'image
Printed in Spain by Graficas Estella
Legal Deposit: October 2009
ISBN: 978-2-81230-137-7
34/2299/5-01